Marijuana Food

Bill Drake

Ronin
Berkeley, CA
www.roninpub.com

Bill Drake

Marijuana Food

Marijuana Food Handbook
ISBN: 0-914171-99-2
Copyright © 1981, 2002 William Drake
All rights Reserved

Published by
RONIN Publishing, Inc.
PO Box 22900
Oakland, CA 94609
roninpub.com

Cover Design: Judy July, Generic Type
                   generictype.com

Distributed to the trade by **Publishers Group West**
Printed in the United States of America by **Bertelsmann**
Library of Congress Card Number: 2002111536

Other books by Bill Drake

The Cultivator's Handbook of Marijuana
The Connoisseur's Handbook of Marijuana
The International Cultivator's Handbook
of Cocaine, Opium, and Hashish
Growing and Curing a Personal Crop
of Natural Tobacco

NOTICE TO READERS

For Lyle

Contents

PART I

Eating
Marijuana
Food

CHAPTER *1*

A Natural, Inexpensive High

It's not as if we haven't tried cooking with marijuana. Ever since Alice Toklas brought marijuana cooking to world attention in the French edition of her famous cookbook, millions of us have tried some variation of the old standby "Dump a lid of cleaned marijuana into a bowl of brownie mix, and bake at 350° for . . ."

I never did have much luck with that sort of brownie. Even if the taste was okay because the marijuana was good, the texture made me expect to wake up with a feedbag on my nose, and each brownie that came out of the pan cost a fortune!

Cooking with natural marijuana extracts changes all that, and also adds great variety to your cooking efforts. Making natural marijuana extracts is a simple matter, and you'll find complete directions later in this book. To begin, however, it's important to understand the difference between extract cooking and the expensive, unsatisfactory chop-and-bake approach—a relatively simple difference, but one with great potential for anyone tired of smoking all the time to get high, but not at all tired of the high experience.

The psychoactive substance THC (tetrahydrocannabinol) is present in natural-state marijuana in both active and inactive forms. Active-form THC amounts to only 10 to 15 percent of the total in a normal leaf. The remaining inactive THC requires heat to render it active, which is why you can't effectively eat or snort marijuana right from the plant. In unsophisticated chop-and-bake marijuana brownie cooking, the heat supplied by the oven changes only a small percentage of inactive THC into active form, so not only is much of the potency wasted, but it also takes a large and expensive amount of marijuana to achieve the high. In smoking, the problem is not the same. In smoking, the heat is supplied by fire, which is very destructive to the THC. A respectable amount does become converted to active form, but smoking is not really a very efficient way to use the wonder herb.

In marijuana extract cooking, not only is the extract prepared beforehand, under optimum temperatures, for the proper amount of time for maximum efficiency of THC conversion, but it is also prepared in the form of either butter, lard, bacon drippings, cream, or as a liqueur, and is then used in cooking whatever dish you desire. Thus with marijuana extracts, you have almost 100-percent efficiency in conversion and availability of marijuana's potency, whereas research shows that a person smoking a joint is lucky to come away with 24 percent of the potential potency, and chop-and-bake marijuana cooking rarely delivers more than 40 percent potential. Cooking with natural marijuana extracts is up to 500 percent cheaper than smoking, and is in every way superior to chop-and-bake cooking.

6-10% up in smoke

50% incinerated

20-22% trapped in roach

18-24% reaches the smoker

Baudelaire's Advice To Hashish Eaters

The great French poet Charles Baudelaire's dramatic and colorful account of his experiences with hashish is offered here as one of the best descriptions ever published of the depth and scope of the marijuana high achieved through eating.

Keep in mind as you read this that Baudelaire's 19th Century hashish was straight from the middle east and was a considerably more powerful form of cannabis than you are likely to find at this time in America—although much of the wonderful, aromatic homegrown sinsemilla available in season is every bit as potent as Victorian hashish.

How Hashish Is To Be Eaten

Common hashish is a decoction of Indian hemp mixed in butter, with possibly a dash of opium. You then have a green sweet, singularly odorous, so odorous in fact that it is somewhat repulsive, an odor at once pervasive & thick.

Taking a nut-sized portion up in a tiny spoon you eat, and are possessed with happiness—an absolute stuporous happiness, a callow happiness of infinite complacency. Such happiness as this lies there for you, in a little morsel of sweet; take it without fear, you won't die of happiness; your physical self cannot be injured gravely by such as this. And if your will comes out of the experience somewhat diminished, that's entirely another concern.

General Rules For Hashish Eaters

In general, to derive from hashish its full force, for a full development of the sensations, you should dissolve it in hot, black coffee taken on an empty stomach; have nothing to eat for ten hours preceding—if you must, have only a light soup.

Infraction of this rule very simply will make you vomit as your dinner quarrels with the drug, and will wipe out the effects of the hashish. Many are the imbecilic & ignorant who, because of rejection of this principle, accuse hashish of being an impotent yet nauseous drug.

You have heard rumors of the marvelous effects of hashish, your imagination has been stimulated by these tales, and you

Towards the end of the soiree, one may eat, but even this activity is not without its difficulties. You experience a great reluctance to stir from your resting place. If your appetite grows to enormous proportions, perhaps you will be able to respond but even then it takes courage to face a bottle of wine, to take up knife & fork.

Getting High Without Smoking

Isn't it interesting how naturally and intimately the ideas of smoking and marijuana go together in our heads? We even talk of "tasting" a little of a friend's homegrown, when most of us really mean rolling those sweet vapors around in our lungs. We are fighting, we believe, for our right to smoke marijuana, free from civil or criminal persecution. What we should be demanding is freedom to use marijuana in any way we choose.

Government studies rarely distinguish between the effects of smoking and the effects of marijuana in their quest for a sign that the killer weed shrinks testicles and causes inverted nipples. Those who fear marijuana wail and assault the reefer (while the righteous, of course, get their own kind of high on Sundays by pressing their tailbones against the tympanic pew, vibrating their backbone with the surge of the organ's sound, and buzzing their brains by droning hymns through the nose). Unfortunately, those who love and defend marijuana claim all too often that dope *smoking* can't possibly do any damage to anyone.

Yet the act of smoking is relatively recent in history. The white world took the act of smoking from the Indians of the New World as greedily as it took the Indians' gold, land, souls, and lives. How the wisest of priests of the New World must have secretly smiled, even as they saw their people melting away. They also saw the white man profanely, haughtily, insatiably inhaling the smoke which invoked the power of their own protective gods, the smoke of tobacco. The Indian priests must have known the destructive force of tobacco abused, known its effects on the greedy whites.

The intricate merging of the idea of smoke with the idea

of marijuana gives us many different clues to our collective psyche, to the assumptions of our culture, our government and its propagandists, and to the potential tyrannical strength of an ingrained concept. If nothing else, the idea of marijuana food will offer a challenge to a basic assumption made about marijuana by both its advocates and its detractors—that you gotta inhale hot gas to get high.

There's no question that marijuana in any form has effects on the body. There's also no question, in the minds of those of us who have been exploring marijuana food, that eating highly potent marijuana extracts is not something best done casually or too frequently. Marijuana foods are a new, different, highly creative form of the marijuana experience when they are used intelligently. If abused, however, they can temporarily be far more incapacitating than a joint, making ordinary tasks very risky.

Still, the many benefits of marijuana foods far exceed the risks of misusing them. Eating marijuana is the ancient, natural way, and if the speedy buzz of the joint can be supplemented or replaced by the gentle, swelling rush of food, then other ancient rhythms might also stir in us. Rhythms of a slower time, when the seas and the winds, the growth of plants, the turning of the sky's objects, the migrations of animals, and the living inner panorama all moved synchronously.

CHAPTER 2

More Advantages of Marijuana Food

The many advantages of eating marijuana begin with the elimination of the little mishaps and hazards all marijuana smokers share. No more little finger dances trying to pass a disintegrating joint for one last toke. No more humping the steering wheel hoping your disco suit doesn't melt while frantically searching your lap for a dropped roach. No more fast switches from toking your homegrown to picking your nose as a highway patrol car pulls up behind you. No more showing up at straight functions trying to seem debonair about smelling like burning alfalfa stubble. No more forgetting where you hid the bag, since most marijuana food is kept in the fridge. No more airing out the house before the babysitter comes, and no more driving in the winter cold with all the windows down to get the smell of ripe Colombian out of the rented car. No more smoking in the bathroom with the exhaust fan on because Mom is coming over. And most wonderful of all, for all of us who have ever had to do it, no more frantic, gagging gobbles of the incriminating contents of the auto's ashtray to the syncopated flash of red and blue lights in the rearview mirror.

Then there is simply relief from the act of smoking. You no longer have to smoke to get high. Much of the initial rush of the smoking high comes not from the THC running 'round your brain, but from instant blood toxicity caused by compounds in the smoke, and from a mild swoon induced by oxygen deprivation. Only after paying this initial price does the body settle down and allow the high itself to come on.

It takes the body a long time to eliminate the effects of even a little marijuana smoking—or of smoking anything, for that matter. With marijuana food, the body has none of the consequences of smoking to deal with. There is no carbon monoxide to inhale, because no burning organic matter is producing those fumes. There are no cancer-causing "tars," since there is no fire to produce them. There are no particles of soot to clog the lungs, no poisons to kill the cells which sweep the lungs clean, no hot gases to damage the tissues of the mouth, throat, and lungs, no heightened acidity in the stomach caused by smoke, no demands on the liver that it cleanse the blood of smoke by-products—in short, none of the ordinary, commonplace physiological pricetags which accompany smoking itself.

Many people have been deciding that smoking anything at all is increasingly interfering with the new, active lifestyle that marks the Eighties. Our bodies can't function cleanly and smoothly after coping with a heavy load of smoke toxins. Exercise demands oxygen, and the blood, heart, and lungs can't keep pace with the demand. Exercise also produces its own natural waste by-products, which the liver, lungs, kidneys, and sweat glands are designed to eliminate. But if these organs are fully occupied dealing with the by-products of smoking, they can't perform their natural functions effectively.

Then, too, the smoking high just doesn't last all that long, and it's a real drag to stop in the middle of an activity to toke up—almost as much of a drag as dealing with the comedown just as you're really getting involved in whatever you're doing. And smoking marijuana is a lot like drinking beer—

only the first one is any good. All the rest progressively lose interest, taste, and effect.

The Marijuana Food High

The marijuana food high is noticeably different from the smoking high, although the essential nature of the high is not altered. The marijuana food high, like the smoking high, opens the doors of perception, increases the range of the senses and enhances their capacities, brings deep places into the light, relieves the mind from fatigue and concern, brings the mysterious inner world into focus, and in many other subtle ways advances the evolution of personal and planetary consciousness.

The characteristics of the high, however, are different. The high is cleaner and clearer. The high is more useful, because it is longer-lasting, and because it is steady. The high requires no reinforcement. It generally does not interfere with vigorous physical activity, although too great a dosage or too-frequent use of marijuana food can interfere with motor coordination. The high has no toxic hangover. The act of eating is, for most, inherently more pleasurable than the act of smoking. Smoking is often self-directed anger, while eating is self-nurturing.

I do want to remind you that moderation is essential to drug use. The marijuana food high is powerful; it demands respect. Just because marijuana food has none of the consequences of the act of smoking doesn't mean that a person can get high on it every day with no ill effects.

But, then, the trade-off between moderate use and daily indulgence is so worthwhile. Who wouldn't trade being high for a whole day, and even evening, once or twice a week for those increasingly obnoxious daily joints or pipes? Or, if you are a person who gets high only infrequently, and already have made a personal decision to be moderate, wouldn't you trade having to smoke all evening to stay high for a few delicious bites of marijuana food at the beginning of the evening, with nothing to do but enjoy yourself for the rest of it?

The marijuana food high comes on in a subtle, delightful way, and takes anywhere from 30 minutes to several hours to enter into awareness. The high creeps up on you, without the rush of smoking. The first sign is a faint suspicion on the edge of consciousness that you may be high. This feeling is akin to the feelings you sometimes get when a storm is approaching, or to the faintly disturbing sensation of déjà vu.

This sort of silently approaching high state can be especially pleasant if you have provided yourself with something enjoyable to do, something which occupies your attention while leaving you totally open to the subtle, oncoming high. It's a real convenience to be able to eat marijuana before going somewhere, and then to go and gradually get high while just standing around sipping mineral water or iced tea. No more doing your Mister Natural walk while slipping out for a joint, and then dropping casually back into the scene, smelling like an old back porch on fire.

The marijuana food high is, for the most part, a very manageable high. A person can plan a good long block of time around being high, long enough to really enjoy, to be productive, creative, to thoroughly get into reading, a play, or a concert.

It's refreshing to be at a party where the level of personal relationships is heightened by marijuana without the atmosphere being polluted by smoke. No more sore throat and metallic tongue at the end of an evening. No more raw eyes (though they still get red). Your lungs, instead of threatening to collapse on you, are ready for a walk, a run, or just a good, clean night's sleep. The food at the party has been tasty because your taste buds haven't been asphyxiated. You've probably been drinking only for taste and pleasure, and not to get high, since you're already nicely there. Perhaps you'll have a glass or two of wine, or a brandy at the end of the meal, but never will you need to drink to get high, and suffer the consequences tomorrow.

You can make marijuana food the centerpiece of an interesting evening by planning when it is to be eaten, what will

be happening as the high comes on, how the period of high is going to be used, and the gentle landing that will end the get-together. (It's important, of course, not to spring mari-juana food on anyone who is unaware that it contains mari-juana.) By planning ahead you'll be able, after a few months' practice, to gauge the portioning and timing of onset of mar-ijuana food for most of your friends. As you and your friends come to know the range of potential of this version of the marijuana high, a marvelous diversity of ways to use it will surely come to you.

Problems for the Law

It's fairly easy to avoid arrest in most places today, as long as you're careful not to attract attention to yourself. As a covert high, marijuana food offers a fascinating set of possi-bilities.

With marijuana food, there's no telltale green vegetable material and seeds left in your possession. Since no visual clues are available, a police officer cannot easily spot you in possession.

Since proper cooking technique can mask the odor of marijuana extract, and since food is normally kept in closed containers, there should be no smell to indicate that the food contains marijuana. Also, there is no smell to give you away while you're eating the food. For instance, if you are sitting on your couch munching a marijuana cookie listening to some nice music and the police come to your door to tell you your car is illegally parked—no problem. You can even be cool and walk to the door munching your cookie to talk with the officer. You might stop short at offering one.

Police need probable cause to detain you and to search for evidence, and they will arrest on the basis of what they find. If you're eating food, how is a police officer to guess that it's marijuana food? Even if you are obviously high, how is the officer to know that you got there by consuming marijuana? You have no alcohol breath, none of the usual alcohol intoxication symptoms—unless you are really stoned. In that case, maybe the cop has reason to stop you, for instance if you are driving a car backwards on the freeway at 70 miles per hour. But if you are just minding your own business, sitting in a park getting high, walking along a trail getting high, skiing getting high, dancing or listening to music getting high, going to school getting high—how is anyone going to be able to say there was reasonable cause to think that the cookie or quiche or sandwich you were eating was getting you high?

There's more. Under most marijuana laws, different amounts of marijuana carry different penalties. Well, how is the Law going to say how much marijuana is in that Thermos of soup you have? Is a bowl of the soup a misdemeanor or a felony? So what if it has 6 grams of THC to a quart? (Whew! That's some soup.) Maybe the butter extract in the soup was made from an ounce of absolutely dynamite marijuana—or maybe it was made with a pound of mediocre roadside weed. One's a misdemeanor most places; one's a felony anywhere. But who is to say which is what, when all they have is the soup? And what legitimate cause did they have to bust the soup in the first place? It is sure to be some kind of legal puzzle.

Narcotics police have been trying for years to come up with

But for God's sake, unless you have an untiring tongue, don't rub marijuana butter all over your partner's body—concentrate on one or two lovely places. Do I have to tell you the places? No, I don't. But let me pass on one true story to show many things: How the exotic gets obscured in the commonplace. How great historical truths are hidden in cliché and cartoon. How much of our common heritage is psychedelic in origin, and how intimately the alteration of consciousness is integrated into the folklore of the ages, but is deliberately obscured.

At the end of October every year, all across the land, tens of thousands of innocents dress up as witches. And what, besides a black cat and a wart on the nose, is the single, most absolutely indispensable piece of witch equipment everyone who cackles must have on All Hallows' Eve? Why, a broomstick, of course. Witches gotta ride broomsticks, right?

Now I'm gonna tell you where that broomstick comes from, friends and neighbors. During the Middle Ages, the dark night of the human soul, there were a lot of people, as there are today, who wanted to know more, see more, feel more of the mysteries of life. Then, as now, some went the route of the church, accepting its promises that endless incantation of holy words and repetition of holy rituals and acceptance of holy authority would bring this revelation.

And then, as now, some relied on their individual courage and rejected the would-be truth-teachings of the many churches, and sought the mysteries themselves. Such people in the Middle Ages were often called witches, and we know that in many places they were burned, dismembered, or otherwise imaginatively and enthusiastically killed.

One of the things that they were burned for was riding their brooms. For in reality, the witch's broom was a smoothly carved stick; in fact, a masturbation instrument which was dipped into a potion made of psychedelic mushrooms and herbs, which the "witch" then rode by masturbation until her vaginal tissues had absorbed the magic elements and her mind flew far beyond the confines of those dark times.

Remember, those were the days, centuries ago, when

lucky new brides were given elaborately embroidered blankets with a single penis-sized hole about two-thirds of the way down the blanket. The idea was that the new bride and groom could get it on on their wedding night without any but the necessary contact—he on top of the blanket, she beneath (natch). You can imagine what such medieval mentality would make of a tripping witch and her magic dildo, carelessly sharing her visions of God as she walked the village green. You can also imagine what the dark urges of such medieval minds would be when given the chance to condemn such adventures into the psyche.

What the witches knew is true. One of the finest places on a woman's body for a marijuana butter massage and tender psychedelic licking is the genitals. As for a man—who is to say not? The penis is also one of the finest places. And if we hear no stories of male witches riding brooms in the Middle Ages, remember that we do hear of sorcerers and their wands. And they, too, were burned by the folks with the little holes in their blankets.

CHAPTER 3

Medical Uses of
Marijuana

You are indeed what you eat, or smoke, and there are lots of reasons to look for that blessed high state through marijuana food rather than through the dull red glow of fire. When you eat marijuana food, you are not only getting high, you are introducing yourself (howdy!) to a high that's been getting plenty of attention lately from pharmaceutical companies, medical researchers, and just plain old doctors.

That recognition, however, takes place largely within a conventional framework. Pharmaceutical megacompanies are saying—Aha, within the plant there are some useful molecules. Let's isolate these molecules, fiddle around with them so that they don't get anyone high (God forbid!), and package them in pills for which we can charge high prices and claim responsibility for the "cures" they produce.

Conventional medicine recognizes that the marijuana plant produces compounds which are useful in treatment of glau-

also recognized cannabis as a stimulating tonic and aphrodisiac, as a specific medicine in asthma, coughs, debility, gout, abdominal swelling, dysentery with blood and fever, in renal colic, bronchitis, fever, and hemorrhoids.

The use of cannabis leaves lightly sautéed in butter and applied warm as an external poultice is common today in rural India and Pakistan for treatment of infection. Such poultices are also commonly used on inflammation or infection of the eyes, ears, nose, or mouth.

In Moslem traditional medicine, cannabis is seen as a useful general tonic, as an agent to promote dryness of the mouth, throat, and lungs in the case of excess phlegm, as an excellent treatment for irritability and nervousness, impotence, and nocturnal emission problems, and as a reliever of neuritis and neuralgia pains, as well as an appetite stimulant.

All the traditional folk medicine systems which recognize the usefulness of cannabis in treating disease, pain, and infection also recognize its properties as a superior euphoriant. In this sense, marijuana food can be a tool of joy.

Granted it's not conventional to think of euphoria as a tool of health and well-being. In fact, naturally euphoric people are often thought of as sick, or at least strange. However, consciously induced and self-directed euphoria is far more than a state of mindless joy. When the euphoriant properties of marijuana are thought of as promoting escapism, they are condemned. Yet in many cases, escape is precisely what a person needs in order to gain first distance, then perspective. When marijuana is used to achieve release from the grip of anxiety, anguish, depression, or other soul-states which are the contemporary plague, who is to say that such release isn't the first step toward facing and dealing with the underlying problems? There is a conventional assumption that people with inner problems should tough it out, and that seeking psychochemical relief is somehow evading their responsibility to suffer until the problem goes away. There is also an assumption that anyone who chooses to get high because life is miserable in some way, or in every possible way, is weak and ineffective. Turning to drugs when life is rough is something only sissies do—real cowboys hang in there, bite the bullet, and sneer at the pain.

One of the remarkable aspects of marijuana's impact on contemporary society is that so many of us have used marijuana as a tool for self-integration without ever actually articulating to ourselves that this is what we've been doing. The impact of marijuana on American consciousness probably can't be accurately assessed now—marijuana is still too controversial for either opponents or proponents to focus on much more than its merit, or lack of merit, as a recreational drug. The role of marijuana in the social, political, economic, and spiritual dimensions of our collective and personal lives does not yet reach far enough across the generations for it to be considered as more than a youth subculture phenomenon —even though many of us who were youths in the sixties are by now closer to male/female menopause than we are to adolescence.

I believe the influence of marijuana on our perspectives, on relationships, on moral, ethical, and spiritual systems, on our material values, our choice of nutrition for body and mind, and our approach to the process of making a living will be seen as immense by future historians. Marijuana use ranks with the great phenomena of the twentieth century as a holistic influence on who we see ourselves to be, why we feel ourselves to be of value and importance, and on our perception of where we are going as a society.

For the Elderly

Old folks who don't already smoke certainly don't need to start, and those who do should probably consider improving the quality of their lives by stopping or cutting down. In either case, marijuana food offers an excellent opportunity for old people to enjoy the unique benefits of marijuana, without smoking. And old people are among those who stand to benefit most from the moderate use of marijuana.

There are very few old people who aren't regularly being ripped off by the many so-called medicines which they believe they have to take. Not only the unnecessary prescription medicines, but all those pain relievers, bowel

uncloggers, mood changers, relaxants, stimulants, and so
forth, that suck money out of old folks' pockets like the black
holes of far space suck in star systems and galaxies. What
most of these folks need is not a medicine chest full of expensive pharmaceutical hocus-pocus, but simply a good tonic.

Back in the last century there were plenty of tonics around
—in fact, that's where most of our contemporary medicine
and drug companies and soft drink companies got their start.
These tonics almost always contained some sort of opiate,
usually morphine, and always had lots of alcohol, which
often contained tincture of cannabis indica. In effect, they
were marijuana liqueurs with an addictive little kicker to
keep the customer coming back. Habitina, an opiate tonic,
bore the solicitous injunction that the user be sure to order
the next month's supply before opening this month's bottle.

Well, that's not exactly what we have in mind here; in fact,
what we're really talking about is not only health but economic independence for old folks. I hope that as older people
discover marijuana they will grow their own, not participate
in the crazy high-priced marijuana market. Over the past 10
years I've heard from several dozen who already do, in Flor-
ida, Arizona, and California. Just as cannabis was a prime
ingredient in the nineteenth-century patent medicines and
tonics, it's being discovered again as an excellent general
tonic.

The aches, pains, ills, and discomforts which accompany
old age are particular favorites of pill companies, not only in
their marketing efforts for current nostrums, but also in their
predictions of future miracle pills. Researchers are busy taking the human body apart looking for sources of natural pain

relievers, stimulants, tranquilizers, aphrodisiacs, and dozens of other chemical compounds manufactured by the brain, glands, nervous system, and other organs. The scope of the market for these future wonder cures is enormous—in the United States alone more than $10 billion is spent annually on pain-relief compounds, more than $13 billion on all manner of proprietary "medicines," most of which are little different from the stuff sold off the tailgate of the medicineman's wagon in the last century.

In contrast to this bewildering assortment of pills, syrups, and capsules, think of marijuana. It is an excellent mood- and mind-altering drug with broad benefits, which is available now and is free to all who grow it themselves. Marijuana cannot be regulated effectively by the government or co-opted by the pharmaceutical companies, and it is as effective an approach to a vast array of human ills as many of the existing or promised pills. It's just a simple plant, but it is here, now, available to anyone who wants it, and it's free, natural, and alive.

So many old folks are sick not from actual disease but from illness of the head and heart, which has more to do with attitude and perception than with disease or degeneration. Cannabis is not a miracle cure, but the old folks I've known who either have discovered it or who have known about it all along (and there are many such) feel that it effectively replaces a wide range of so-called medicines, and that it's fun besides. New or enhanced interest in sex, food, ideas, relationships—the possibilities of life—characterize the response of many old people to cannabis.

In Cancer Therapy

Marijuana is getting much attention as an effective anti-nausea agent for people receiving chemotherapy and radiation treatments for cancer. The government is moving very slowly on this matter, perhaps because of a built-in reluctance to say anything good about the weed which has been the object of its institutionalized hatred for so long. Even in the states which have managed to make marijuana legal for medical purposes, many hundreds of patients are in agony rather than receiving relief because the government insists on an absurd system of multiple endorsements by doctors, narcotics police, and bureaucrats for marijuana therapy. Of course, many people will have no trouble finding or growing their own marijuana, and using it. I believe that this independent approach is best, rather than waiting forever for the government's "permission" to seek relief from pain. Cancer patients in many states have experimented with our processes and recipes with remarkable results. Not only do these folks report that the marijuana they eat is much more effective in relieving pain and nausea than marijuana they have been smoking, but also that their bodies, already in jeopardy and under great toxic assault, no longer need to put up with any further insult from hot gas and toxic smoke. Also, the marijuana food high lasts three to four times longer than the high achieved by smoking.

In many states, of course, the prescribed treatment is not to smoke a government joint but to receive a government injection of THC extract or to swallow a capsule of THC oil. Not much fun, and still not as effective as eating a nice portion of some tasty marijuana food.

In a children's hospital in a great western city there is a cancer ward. It is a painful place to be, not only for the children suffering actual physical agony, but also for the parents who must watch helplessly while their children are dragged through merciless hell, for the doctors and nurses who must confront the death and destruction of this brightest, most poignant form of human life, and for those of us who for whatever reason find ourselves visiting a child in this relentless place. It is also a place where one can watch little children smoking one joint after another, in order to receive relief from the other side of suffering—the agony of chemotherapy.

Within 10 years there is great promise that cancer can be treated by extracts of the human body's own cancer-fighting agents, such as interferon, but until that sort of treatment becomes available, many people with cancer are still going to be given massive doses of painful poisons in an attempt to kill the cancerous part of their body without killing the normal part. The pain resulting from this differential destruction of their tissues and the nausea resulting from chemotherapy can only be dealt with in certain ways. Food made with marijuana, while relatively unknown, seems to be at least as effective as other forms of relief.

In the days immediately following chemotherapy, most patients can keep no food down, and so marijuana food is still not a practical solution to this most painful stage of post-therapy. Smoking a joint is one of the few forms of relief available. It's disheartening irony to see a small child sucking on a joint in order to quell the hellish turmoil in his little insides. But after a day or two, when the child's body has calmed, is there any further need to continue smoking a joint every few hours? Some doctors are beginning to think not. Once a child can keep a marijuana cookie down, he receives six or eight hours of clean, smokeless relief instead of the one or two hours of toxic relief a joint affords. And if, we pray, the chemotherapy takes hold and works, the child still suffers pain, and there are few better drugs for pain than marijuana —not that it masks the pain or makes it seem to go away, as some drugs do, but it creates in a person's mind an alternative state of consciousness in which there is both pain relief and an openness to other forms of experience. A person who is confronted with death, whether at an early age or an advanced age, needs access to all forms of consciousness. Marijuana food can open the door to various levels of consciousness and allow the patient to explore them.

Government Research

Extensive clinical/epidemiological studies in Jamaica and India fail to show any clear-cut set of unavoidable negative consequences of marijuana use. Current government-sponsored research is inconclusive at best when it speaks of marijuana's harmful effects. Extensive popular experience supports the concept that nothing about marijuana itself is inevitably adverse.

> The evaluation of the pharmacological activity of smoked hashish or marijuana (of known quality) cannot be made independently of the conditions of the smoking process.
>
> The amount of the active constituents introduced into the organism after the smoking of cannabis preparations depends also on the dryness of the preparation (marijuana or hashish), the current of air passed through (current of oxygen), the temperature of combustion, etc.
>
> If one considers the great differences in the quantity and the quality of the active cannabinols (and isomers, etc.) which are contained in the various cannabis preparations produced according to miscellaneous techniques (time of maturation, variety of plants) all over the world, in addition to the problems in connection with the smoking process, the great conflict about the action of cannabis on human smokers can be easily understood.
>
> —United Nations Research
> Report, *Effects of the*
> *Smoking Process on Cannabis*
> *Constituents*

Government-sponsored marijuana research has confused what little reasoned debate has existed on the subject. Most marijuana research begins with a fundamental assumption that we're dealing with something of the proportion and character of the Black Death. Thus, any consideration of marijuana's medicinal effects is clouded by complex reactions that mix fear, prejudice, and ignorance. It's not just marijuana that provokes such intense confusion of medical and nonmedical considerations—look at the storm over the different breast cancer surgery techniques; look at the debate over the effectiveness of laetrile on cancer; look at the heat generated between advocates and opponents of pulling the plug when brain death has occurred. Past events as well as current events generate examples of the general human propensity to confuse the medical and nonmedical sides of an issue. Look at the ban on coffee consumption in Europe when it was first introduced from the New World. For decades coffee was feared .by some, and secretly gulped by others, as a profound mind-altering drug whose effects were, depending on your point of view, certain either to end civilization in Europe or to result in a wave of enlightenment across the Western world.

The difference between the role of government in marijuana research and in many of these other instances is that in marijuana research, the government has taken an a priori position—it wants to find something horrible in marijuana, and it assumes that something horrible is there to be found.

Elsewhere in the book I cite the most obvious piece of evidence of governmental prejudice in this matter—the general failure of such research to distinguish between the effects of smoking and the effects of marijuana, lumping everything together in an undisguised, unsophisticated smear campaign. What is less obvious at first glance is the government's sponsorship of one kind of high—the alcohol high—and attempted government suppression of another kind of high—the marijuana high. That people have an intrinsic right to choose their high is not recognized, and massive governmental effort has been directed at proving that marijuana is a dangerous, undesirable high—contrary to the experience of those who choose it.

That's an important point. It's unlikely that a definitive experiment or piece of research will show marijuana itself to be bad or especially dangerous, although marijuana smoking will certainly become recognized as a dangerous form of use. Over time, a collective popular wisdom regarding drugs has gathered, and marijuana has been chosen as a drug of great value. I think it's likely that marijuana will ultimately enter the mainstream of our culture as the recreational drug of choice, replacing alcohol, and will then come to enjoy not only full legal status, but also all the accompanying hype and commercial exploitation.

Use by Children?

A marijuana issue which masquerades as medical but which is largely emotional is the use of marijuana by children. Parents who fear marijuana see it as a potential cause of harm or disaster for their children. Parents' imaginations habitually roam their children's future looking for danger, and for many parents drugs are seen as evil embodied, with a will of their own and with the intent to do harm to those foolish enough to use them.

Marijuana use is feared to be the most common form of drug use by young people, though many professional drug counselors see alcohol abuse as a far more serious problem both for children and adults. Some children are going to be physically or psychologically damaged by any recreational drug, including marijuana. You can't tell in advance who these kids are going to be. You can't even tell while it's going on—to know for sure, you would have to be able to look into the future. A heavy-smoking heavy-drinking sexually promiscuous 15-year-old might become a balanced, healthy, creative 35-year-old, and a pure, bright prospect at 15 may turn into a thrice-divorced suicidal mid-30s speed-freak wipeout.

Nobody would argue that the healthy development of young or old people is enhanced by immoderate and unrestricted drug use, and all would agree that some people, young or old, will have a negative response to any recreational substance—whether it's marijuana, alcohol, tobacco, sugar, coffee, Valium, opium, cocaine, or cola drinks. Nobody can tell if another person is going to get into trouble by taking any of these substances for recreational purposes, or for any reason. We all know people who've grown up on a strict junk-food diet, who smoke, drink, stay up late, and use swear words, who are in great physical, emotional, and mental health—and others, who, in spite of sprouts, mantras, and good thoughts, are an absolute wreck.

The fact is that millions of people regularly use marijuana with the healthy ease and sense of balance of a connoisseur enjoying a good wine or tasty meal, and that there are other millions who use marijuana with the self-destructive, negative attitude of a wino or compulsive overeater. The difference must lie within the person, not as an attribute of what the person consumes. No one wants his or her child to be the wino rather than the connoisseur, but too many parents are ready to believe that if their child has even one experience

with marijuana, there is something in the marijuana itself which will grab the child and destroy him. Nonsense it is, but powerful nonsense, because few parents want to admit that it is the child who is responsible for his or her own life, and that if the child turns out to have a drug problem, it is the doing of the child, not the drug. Yet, without such a realization, and without a willingness to cease placing blame anywhere, and especially not on the drug, no parent of a child in trouble will be able to help that child.

The government bears major responsibility for the confusion suffered by parents of children in drug trouble, because government propaganda has spent years of effort and millions of dollars trying to convince people that marijuana has the intrinsic power to corrupt. Who can blame a parent who believes that the drug causes the problem? And who can blame anyone, much less a child, who is fascinated by the images of lurking evil and who, upon trying marijuana and discovering that it is not only not evil, but fun, then decides that there must be nothing at all wrong with using it any time, any place?

I'm a parent, and I share with all parents a hope that my child will not get into drugs at least until he is old enough to appreciate the good sense of moderation and respect for the integrity of his mind and body. But when the time comes that he does want to try marijuana, I am going to recommend that he use it in the ancient way by eating it, rather than smoking it—and then I'm going to have to hope that he will listen and agree with me, because I will have no power at all to forbid him one way or another.

CHAPTER *4*

Mainstream Marijuana

Ten years ago the only place you could find papers and screens was in funky head shops in the big bad cities. Now you can buy brass waterpipes at gift shops in every suburban shopping center. Ten years ago, any sleezy narc could get a write-up in the paper and a commendation from the boss for busting three adolescents sucking on a joint in the alley behind their parents' garage; today there have to be 50 tons in the shipment before it even rates a note on page 12. Yesterday it was a matter of principle to smoke a joint before every class; today a lot of folks save it for Saturday.

Marijuana has long since ceased to be the almost exclusive domain of social outcasts. It has moved through the long period of its secret infiltration of the minds and bodies of the white kids in middle class land. It has transcended tyrannical attempts to suppress it, scientific assaults on its genes, mad propaganda diatribes, and official warnings that even an instant's folly with it will lead to desperate acts of robbery and violence as the addict vainly seeks to keep pace with the growth of his disgusting habit.

My, my. With all those marijuana addicts leaping out of alleys onto the backs of helpless citizens, the street should be strewn with carcasses. Unless the sanitation department has increased 1000 percent in effectiveness, something's wrong, 'cause the body count just doesn't sustain the official line.

For years now, researchers have been probing away at the brains of THC-fried mice and strangely willing bearded human subjects, trying to discover the secret of all that music, color, and warmth generated within. You can bet they would have yelled fire pronto if they had discovered anything on their recording devices but the tracings of tranquility and insight.

Well, just as marijuana smoke has had profound effects on America, marijuana food stands to have at least an equal impact, and incidentally to provide the researchers with a whole new field of play. Imagine the thrill government-sponsored researchers will feel when they realize that not only do they now have to investigate marijuana food, but they also have to test whether or not marijuana cookies wreak the same havoc on the degenerate addict's body as does Fettuccine à la Santa Marta. Quel problème!

The Working Folks' High

An awful lot of us would rather work high than try to do our jobs day after day with a straight head. Executives and managerial-level people have no problem stepping out at lunch for a few drinks, getting a nice buzz on for the rest of the afternoon. Of course, working folks can drink at lunchtime too, but the opportunities for lower-level employees to get high on alcohol at lunch are limited.

Besides, an alcohol high really isn't that pleasant. An hour or so after you get back on the job, you need a boost, or else you have to put up with a hangover between three o'clock and five. That's why so many upper-echelon folks stay well into the afternoon at business lunches—their unconscious timing tells them that unless they keep drinking until at least 2:30, they are going to have a hard time of it until 4:30.

With marijuana food, working folks can enjoy a mellow and manageable high that lasts nicely through the day. A small amount of marijuana food, eaten just before starting work, say, at 8:20 A.M., will come on between 9 and 10 and will last through the morning and well into the afternoon. After work is your own time, and you may want to start that part of the day with a fresh head. An alternative, of course, is to take another little portion of marijuana food around one to two o'clock, so that the high can begin coming on just as your morning snack is wearing off. With this arrangement, a working person can stay high all day, without smoking before work, and without having to sneak off for a joint during work to get a high which doesn't last that long.

How much better to come to work, settle down into some pleasant task, and allow the high to come on gradually as you really get into whatever you're doing. The lunch break comes at the ideal time during such a high. You are able to relax and use the hour for enjoyment of food and conversation, for a walk, for reading, or for simply thinking.

After lunch, with the light high extended into the afternoon, and with food inside you nourishing you and giving you energy, you can work contentedly for the rest of the afternoon.

Of course, some work—such as those jobs involving driving, using machinery, and lab work—is not really conducive to being high on marijuana or anything else, and each person will have to decide if there are risks too great to tolerate. But most jobs are routine and risk-free, and are done equally well by people who are mellow and relaxed as by people who are uptight and running scared—those whom the bosses call "motivated employees." Bosses have never liked drugs for anyone but themselves. Marijuana has presented a particular problem to bosses of all kinds, because it has long been recognized that the marijuana high makes people quite difficult to manage. For one thing, many of us move more slowly when we are high on marijuana; we're less aggressive, less motivated by material reward, less tolerant of authoritarian bullshit, more vocal about bad working conditions and bad supervision, more interested in our own lives than the job, less afraid of threats of punishment, job loss, and so forth, more open to solidarity of interest with fellow workers, slower to do what the bosses want us to do, and generally behave in ways that make bosses uneasy.

It's no wonder that drugs in general, and marijuana in particular, are such a threat to the way of life which bosses have established for themselves. The games don't work when workers are high. The bosses can't or won't restructure their way of employing people to do work, so it's up to the working people to change themselves, if they will and if they can.

Eating marijuana food is the best way to be high on the job for most people. Lunchboxes of America unite! You have nothing to lose but your lids.

The Marijuana Food Biz

The marijuana business is a multibillion dollar affair as it is, but it does have one distinct drawback: Raw marijuana is not only bulky and obvious, it is open to detection by any halfwit who has ever taken the trouble to know what the stuff looks or smells like. Not only is it difficult to transport and sell, but it is also risky to handle and keep.

Marijuana food promises to change all that. And it's a simple matter to set up food-producing facilities in the areas where marijuana is grown, convert the marijuana to any of dozens of food products which mimic straight foods, and bring these products into the country, in the case of foreign-grown marijuana, or distribute them throughout the country, in the case of domestically grown marijuana, with far less risk of detection than you would run dealing in raw marijuana.

Those people whose joy and reason for being is to walk around docks and airports with dope-sniffing animals on a leash will find their task immensely complicated by marijuana food. While, granted, the odor of marijuana food de-

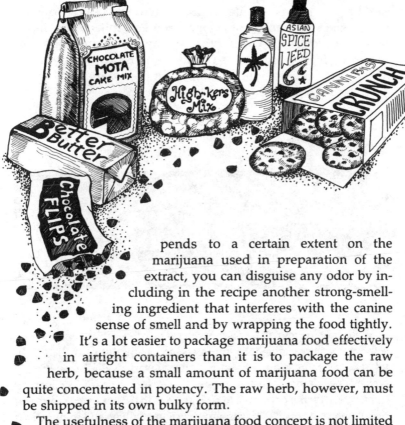

pends to a certain extent on the marijuana used in preparation of the extract, you can disguise any odor by including in the recipe another strong-smelling ingredient that interferes with the canine sense of smell and by wrapping the food tightly.

It's a lot easier to package marijuana food effectively in airtight containers than it is to package the raw herb, because a small amount of marijuana food can be quite concentrated in potency. The raw herb, however, must be shipped in its own bulky form.

The usefulness of the marijuana food concept is not limited to shipping across borders. In several West Coast cities people have discovered that a Friday afternoon route in a few high-rise office buildings can be very profitable, and is as safe as the discretion of the person who sets up the route makes it. On the surface such a route will appear to be no more than an ordinary snack service, complete with the usual sort of office worker munchy foods. I know of one such office route, which served well over a hundred regular customers on Friday afternoon. Office workers had their cookie delivered about two in the afternoon, nibbled away without arousing the least suspicion, and by the end of the day were nicely high and ready to boogie all Friday night.

Marijuana food delivery services can be developed in a number of places besides office buildings. Large public events such as concerts offer opportunities; folks in the military who offer such a service to their comrades-in-arms would be highly appreciated, and perhaps a roving vendor at a public beach would succeed. The possibilities are open for those with fertile imaginations, and gardens.

For Your Bones

While looking into dietary issues related to osteoporosis I came across some amazing research done in Finland on a natural sugar called Xylitol. This research strongly suggests that dietary Xylitol cannot only prevent development of osteoporosis, it can reverse existing osteoporosis by causing new bone material to be laid down in the hollowed out spaces of osteoporotic bones. This research has potentially useful implications for people suffering bone density loss from either osteoporosis or other causes such as chemotherapy. This research also says that people recovering from bone breaks, including broken hips, can benefit greatly from the addition of Xylitol sugar to their diet, simply by replacing their granulated Sucrose with granulated Xylitol and introducing other Xylitol products like chewing gum and mouthwash into their daily routine.

Xylitol is a sweet, fresh-tasting pure white sugar that looks and tastes just like granulated cane sugar and can be used in place of cane sugar in any of the recipes in this book. If anything it's a little sweeter than cane sugar, although not nearly as sweet as granulated fructose. It is produced mainly in Finland, where it is extracted from Birch trees just like

Maple syrup is extracted from Sugar Maple trees in the Northern United States. Finland produces over 50% of the world's relatively tiny supply of natural Xylitol, and the only place that Americans are likely to run across it is in a few brands of toothpaste & mouthwash (Tom's products) and chewing gum (Ford Gum Company).

Initial scientific research interest in Xylitol was stimulated by the observation that the Lapp people living in rural Northern Finland almost never got cavities. By examining their lifestyle it became apparent that they used fresh twigs from birch trees to scrub and pick their teeth after meals. Finnish scientists discovered that Xylitol actually reverses cavities – regular daily use of Xylitol chewing gum causes the holes to re-mineralize. It also reverses gum disease and cures low-grade jaw/ear infections that are a common side effect of bad teeth.

The question naturally arises—if curing or preventing osteoporosis and other diseases caused by poor absorption of minerals and nutrients,

and if preventing dental disease as well, is a simple matter of replacing the cane sugar in my diet with Xylitol, why isn't this stuff on every grocery store shelf and in every food product, soft drink, packaged cereal, and candy bar in the US?

The simple answer is that the global sucrose/fructose sugar interests are politically very powerful and they are fully invested in cane sugar and fructose production land and facilities worldwide. They have absolutely no intention of allowing you or me to have easy access to Xylitol in our diets because they have no way of producing it or controlling it, and they are afraid that if word about Xylitol gets out their enormous worldwide empire could collapse. So all in all the motivation of the global sugar interests is straightforward and easily understood- greed and fear.

This is in spite of the fact that for people who are at risk for, or who are currently experiencing bone demineralization Xylitol may be a partial or complete solution at a cost of literally pennies per day. For people undergoing chemotherapy, the inclusion of Xylitol in a diet that includes Soy and fresh vegetables and fruits could make the difference between extended suffering and a quick return to health. For elderly people at great risk for hip and back fractures a few months of Xylitol in a diet rich with Soy and fresh foods could begin to actually heal their weakened skeletal frames.

For people who cannot quit smoking or heavy drinking, and who may not care to eat a healthy diet, the inclusion of Xylitol in snack foods of all kinds could have a major preventative public health impact and reduce long range public costs dramatically. Xylitol is even well-tolerated by many diabetics, according to the research, because it is absorbed slowly throughout the gut rather than quickly in the upper gut like sucrose, fructose or dextrose. This means that diabetics may actually be able to enhance their absorption of food nutrients by the inclusion Xylitol in their diets.

So as you browse the recipes in this book keep in mind that if you are using Marijuana to deal with health issues, you may be smart to include Xylitol in your diet as well.

Traveling High

The government usually starts advertising around May each year that "If you get busted overseas, you're in for the hassle of your life." It obviously hopes to reach people just before summer vacation time, when most of us travel. Not a word in the ads, of course, that the main reason why you stand to get busted overseas is because the U.S. government has been encouraging and equipping foreign governments to bust people for marijuana and other fiendishly dangerous substances. Still, the warning is valid, as any of us who have ever seen the insides of a Mexican or North African jail can humbly testify. In one year, for instance, 1466 Americans were busted overseas for possession of an ounce or less of marijuana.

So people still travel with dope, hoping not to get busted at any of the borders one must cross when on a trek. Traveling in another country while high is a wonderful experience. The natural high of travel, the sense of freedom and wonder at the strangeness of the surroundings, the impact of the sights, sounds, and smells of unusual places, foods and circumstances, the delightful freedom most of us feel when we enter into conversation with strangers from other countries, the expansion of perspective and perception which is stimulated by traveling—all of these experiences and many others are enhanced by being nicely, alertly, vibrantly high. That's why so many of us risk the hassle of our lives and carry marijuana with us while traveling.

I can't help wondering if Paul McCartney would have been busted in Japan if, instead of trying to get ½ pound of marijuana into that tight little island by carrying a plastic bag full in his luggage, he had been carrying a tin of cookies. Because that's the point—travelers routinely carry all kinds of food with them, and the same difficulties present themselves to a customs cop in another country as present themselves to a cop here when confronted by marijuana food. If there is no visible evidence, no smell—how is anyone going to suspect that the food in your pack or suitcase is contraband? When marijuana food is properly prepared with marijuana that does not impart that peculiar barnyard odor to the food, or when that odor is disguised (I explain how on p. 92), traveling high ought to be pretty safe for us all.

There's no guarantee—let's be clear on that. Marijuana food does not ensure against arrest and prosecution—it just lessens the odds that an individual who is cool in all other ways will be challenged at the border.

Marijuana Food and Craftspeople

There are probably very few craftspeople who don't already know about marijuana and who have not already decided whether it's a good drug to use while working. But for those who have decided that it is a good thing, marijuana food has some special benefits, and for those who have decided against smoking marijuana while working, marijuana food may hold promise worth exploring.

In the case of craftspeople who feel positively about use of marijuana in their craft, the principal benefit is the marijuana food high's much longer duration. It is definitely a drag on creativity to have to keep toking every several hours just to stay high, and the quality of the high is diminished with each successive joint, so the effort becomes a struggle as the day or evening wears on. With the six- to eight-hour high available with marijuana food, sustained-high creative effort becomes a reality. In addition, the mind is much clearer because of the absence of smoke toxins in the system.

For some people, motor coordination is impaired by marijuana food to a greater degree than with smoking. Depending on the artist's craft, then, marijuana food for creative activity may involve some risk. It may be more appropriate for the cerebral crafts such as writing and painting, and less appropriate for those that require the use of potentially dangerous tools, such as woodworking or welding. It may be that marijuana food is more appropriate during the period of inspiration and less appropriate during the period of execution. Then, too, there are idiosyncratic factors involved in artistic creativity—there will be some times when marijuana, whether smoked or eaten, will work for a person and other times when it will block—with no apparent pattern to its effect.

Marijuana has been a traditional accompaniment to artistic creativity in many of the ancient cultures in India and Persia, and the creative professions most commonly using the holy herb have been those requiring sustained concentration, such as jewelry making, or sustained repetitive effort, such as weaving, or sustained inspiration, such as poetry. Each creative professional will seek and find her or his own relationship with mind-altering agents, and that's how it should be.

PART II

Making Marijuana Extracts

CHAPTER 5

Before You Begin . . .

My interest in marijuana food goes back to when I was writing *The Connoisseur's Handbook of Marijuana* in 1970–71, traveling in North Africa and the East, experiencing for the first time some of the traditional marijuana preparations such as majoum, alwa candy, and churum.

Churum, an ancient dish which I first tasted in Geneva, prepared for me by a Turkish friend and scholar, is a sweet, pungent dish of brown rice, coconut chips, spices, and marijuana butter. It's served cold, can be wonderfully potent, and is also delicious. Alwa candy is a traditional Indian confection of sugar, rose petals, spices, dried figs, and butter. And majoum, found all around the eastern and southern Mediterranean, is a delicious sort of marijuana brittle which is wonderful eaten fresh, but better when aged a week or so. Recipes for these and other such goodies are found in my *Connoisseur's Handbook of Marijuana* (1971).

After eating these traditional foods during my research trips, I came home and began experimenting with the recipes. It became clear to me that butter played a key role in the recipes, since the butter and the marijuana were always together, usually heated together for a period of time. The next step was to try to produce a simple extract of marijuana using butter, which I first did in late 1971. It wasn't a difficult process at all, and after that I occasionally made up a batch of cookies using marijuana butter. Once in a while I tried my hand at a holiday treat like alwa candy.

But it was not until 1978 that I began experimenting seriously, not only with butter, but with other kinds of fat (animal and vegetable) in an attempt to see just how versatile this means of getting high could be. I was prompted to experiment by a growing conviction that I had to stop smoking, and by the certainty that I did not want to stop being high.

In the next two chapters you'll learn many ways to prepare marijuana extracts for cooking, but that doesn't mean that all the extraction processes are known. In the course of several years, those of us who have been playing with marijuana extract cooking have been able to discover a number of very effective extract bases, such as bacon drippings, which have never been suggested before. We'll also cover other processes of our own creation, such as alcohol bath butter extraction, which we've found to be effective and versatile. If, as you're playing with the processes which follow, you discover an angle or a trick you want to pass along, then please do. And if you aren't so much into the art, sport, and pastime of cooking, then just pick some marijuana foods you enjoy —and enjoy.

Marijuana Food Overdose

As a general rule, it's easier to overdose on marijuana food than it is to overdose by smoking—unless you do an entire joint of two-toke by yourself, or something equally delightful but foolish. With smoking there's an almost immediate feedback from your body, and it's possible to gauge the intensity of the high pretty closely while you're smoking. With marijuana food, you can eat *far* too much and not begin to realize it for an hour or so, by which time the potency has been absorbed by your body and is well on its way toward saturating your nerve net. With smoking you can keep track of the high as you go, but with marijuana food you have to control your dosage up front.

The marijuana overdose is normally not dangerous, but it can be very unpleasant. In the first place, the overdose involves two sets of symptoms. The first set is simply excessive THC running around the brain. The second set of symptoms usually results from low blood sugar, or transient hypoglycemia (most of us know it as the "blind munchies").

The body, put into low-sugar shock by the effects of marijuana on organs and glands, develops a gnawing sharp-toothed urge for sugary foods, like candy, sweet wine, grains, fruits, and baked goodies. In mild hypoglycemic reactions, brought about by moderate marijuana use by a healthy person, there are few symptoms other than the munchies, although some of the other parts of the high can be traced to low blood sugar rather than to THC. The occasional dizzy, disoriented feelings we experience, the listlessness and difficulty in concentrating—these are sensations which accompany hypoglycemia. They do not really belong to the high state itself.

When you overdose on marijuana food, you are likely to experience not only a profound marijuana high which is incapacitating, but also a serious hypoglycemic reaction. This means that, for some people, a marijuana overdose can create a definite life hazard. If someone has undiagnosed diabetes, chronic hypoglycemia, kidney or liver problems, or other similar problems, too much marijuana in any form can be dangerous. Again, smoking too much can produce equally serious dangers for some people. It's just not as likely that a person will involuntarily overdose on smoking.

The ideal preventative course would be to put a giant sign on any marijuana food you prepare (see illustration). If you could be sure everyone could read, heed, and understand the sign, there would be very little chance of anyone having an accidental overdose. However, it might not be practical for you to keep your marijuana food in such obvious fashion. But unless you do, you create the possibility that someone

will inadvertently eat your stash and get straight-staring horizontally high.

Another way to deal with the problem is to make only food you can hide—like cookies. But hidden cookies, if found, create a potentially serious problem, since anyone finding a cookie stash is almost honor-bound to eat at least half the stash. It happened to a good friend. She came home one afternoon to find her grandmother, and the dear old lady's two equally dear little old blue-haired friends, all overwhelmingly high, and not at all sure they liked their situation. By later count, these senior trippers had consumed 17 cookies between them—cookies which were each supposed to be single-dose potency.

The first thing this friend did was to level with the ladies about what had happened and to reassure them that—despite their pounding hearts, intense mental experiences, and inability to coordinate thought, speech, or limbs—they were going to be okay. She then suggested that they might even try to enjoy the experience. With that, her grandmother, a lady known to be able to resist the impact of many formidable martinis, rose out of her slump from the sofa, strode—not walked—to the cookie jar, and said, "Well then, darling, why don't you eat a couple of your damn cookies and join us!" Which she did.

Treating an Overdose

The overdose situation described above turned out all right —but it's easy to visualize other situations with not-so-acceptable results. Once you are in the middle of an overdose, there is very little you can do other than relax and try to enjoy it or focus on something other than the high. Many who are experienced with drugs know that it is possible to separate your consciousness and its controls from the high state by a combination of relaxation and concentration. It's not easy to function normally while dealing with an overdose, but the more experienced you are the better you can cope, or help another person cope.

It also helps if the person who has overdosed consumes readily assimilable protein rather than speedy carbohydrates like sugar. The protein, as it is broken down during digestion into its simpler elements, will serve as a source of carbohydrates the body needs to bring the blood sugar back into balance. And in the time it takes the body to digest the protein, its balance will be restored gradually instead of being whipped through swift blood-sugar changes. In fact, a light broth such as chicken soup, along with some simple brown rice or whole-wheat toast, forms a near-perfect nutritional compensation for an overdose. Most people will have to wait 30 to 60 minutes after the first heavy waves of an overdose before they can even think about eating. But a light snack like the one described (along with a banana, papaya, or melon, for potassium) will go a long way toward relieving the overdose symptoms associated with hypoglycemic shock to the system. Also, the simple act of eating gives one a sense of being restored, and enables a more positive attitude toward the experience.

A really profound overdose can leave a person high off and on for days, the high often accompanied by unpleasant body sensations. Overdose is not in itself dangerous, though it can be if the person is not healthy to begin with or tries to drive or perform other risky tasks. A physician's assistance should always be considered in the case of an overdose.

Also, almost all states have toll-free confidential poison control phone numbers. You can reach a poison control clearinghouse by dialing 1-800-555-1212 and asking the operator for emergency assistance in reaching a poison control center. Also, increasing numbers of cities offer emergency 911 dialing or its equivalent. It's a good move to find out what your local resources are.

The mental state of someone going through an overdose is perhaps the most critical factor. If a person panics, the body goes rigid on a deep level, the trip becomes more difficult than it would otherwise be, and the chances for damage are increased. If a victim can develop a positive mental attitude soon after the discovery of the overdose and can be aware of what is happening without being afraid or dominated by it psychologically, then the overdose will be as easy as it can be. Fortunately, marijuana is a relatively benign drug, even in overdose form. Any basically healthy person can cope with and live through a marijuana food overdose, or an overdose caused by smoking. It's just real unpleasant, and not likely to be done more than once.

After this long, precautionary discussion, you may be feeling so nervous about marijuana food that you'll decide it's time to toke up on a nice, fat joint. Well, go right ahead. But unless you've got some strong reason to worry, like diabetes or one of the other problems just covered, while you're smoking that joint make up a batch of marijuana extract, using one of the following techniques. You may just find that this joint is the last one you'll want to smoke for a long while.

CHAPTER **6**

Basic Butter Extracts

Butter is the ancient, traditional solvent for THC, and it's a very efficient absorber of the sacred molecule indeed. Almost all traditional marijuana food recipes from India, Persia, Turkey, Morocco, and elsewhere utilize butter as the extract base.

Marijuana butter extract, prepared in any one of the ways covered here, can be used in literally thousands of recipes. Its color may occasionally limit its usefulness, and for those occasions you will no doubt want to experiment with the other interesting and effective bases described. By and large, however, butter is the most useful extract base.

The most basic THC extraction process is water bath extraction using butter as the base. This process takes advantage of the fact that THC is soluble in fats, such as butter, but not in water. Use the water bath technique to extract relatively large amounts of marijuana with relatively small amounts of butter, in order to concentrate the THC. Thus if you have a crop of homegrown which has to be harvested early due to sudden security problems, you may want to concentrate the potency of a large amount of not-quite mature marijuana in a small amount of butter. Or, if your marijuana is perfectly fine and you have no desire to concentrate its potency, you can just cook up a large amount of nice, mellow butter using the water bath method.

Calculating Proportions of Extract Base to Marijuana

If you're working with a very high-potency marijuana, a little marijuana will make a lot of extract. If, on the other hand, you're working with marijuana so weak that you can't smoke enough to get high without nausea, you'll need a lot of marijuana for a small amount of extract base.

Whether marijuana is strong or weak to you will depend on how susceptible you are to the holy high state, on how the marijuana is smoked or eaten, and on other factors. In addition, there are no objective home tests for potency, so you're stuck with subjectivity. You can get esoteric if you want, and do things like putting several dozen ants into a jar, blowing it full of marijuana smoke, and counting the frequency of 360° circles among those ants still walking. If only we had something like a litmus paper test for potency!

Ah, well, anyone who's reasonably experienced with marijuana can divide it into three or four categories of potency. So let's establish a subjective scale of potency for the purpose of discussing batch potency in marijuana extract preparation.

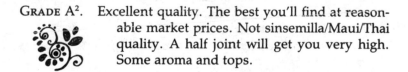

GRADE A[1].   Extremely potent. When smoked it is definitely two-toke. It may be very fine, aromatic, resin-flavored sinsemilla, or Thai-stick quality, or very heavy Colombian with that barnyard aroma.

GRADE A[2].   Excellent quality. The best you'll find at reasonable market prices. Not sinsemilla/Maui/Thai quality. A half joint will get you very high. Some aroma and tops.

GRADE B. Moderate quality. Competent but not excellent homegrown or bulk imported stuff. It takes one or two joints to get you high for several hours. Probably gives you a headache. Little aroma, few tops.

GRADE C. Found along roads in the Midwest; also growing in homes with poor light, poor soil, excess watering, etc. You can't smoke enough to get high without getting sick.

Okay—with these subjective grades established, let's talk about marijuana/extract base proportions. We'll use butter as the example.

With the very best marijuana, Grade A¹, use a ratio of 1 ounce of marijuana to 16 to 20 oz. butter. This will yield 100 to 125 teaspoons of very potent extract, each of which will produce a six- to nine-hour high.

With Grade A² use a ratio of 1 ounce marijuana to 12 to 16 oz. butter for a yield of 75 to 100 teaspoons of potent extract, each one good for a five- to eight-hour high.

For Grade B marijuana, a ratio of 1 ounce of marijuana to 8 ounces of butter works the best. This yields 50 teaspoons of extract, each one potent enough for four to seven hours of high times.

Grade C marijuana—the dregs—is still just fine for extract preparation, as long as you use a high marijuana-to-butter ratio. Try 1 ounce of marijuana to 4 ounces of butter or several ounces of marijuana to 1 stick of butter. Since you are using so little butter, you will have to use the water bath extract technique.

You can make larger batches of marijuana butter simply by doubling or tripling the amounts given here. As long as you keep your ratio of marijuana to butter constant—1:16 or 1:20 for Grade A¹, 1:12 for Grade A², 1:8 for Grade B, and so on —the potency of the marijuana butter will not be changed. Of course, as soon as you change the ratio, you will produce a higher or lower potency extract.

A terrific approach used by two of my thriftier buddies is

to ask their friends to save seeds and stems for them. Once a month or so they make their rounds, collecting the marijuana trash their friends have no use for. Of course, a situation in which everybody wins is better than one person's taking advantage of another, so my two friends always bake up the extract they prepare from this discarded marijuana trash into cookies, which they share with those who shared with them. With seeds and stems, you'll want to use a high ratio of marijuana to butter—my friends find that 1½ pounds of marijuana trash produces a very nice 6 to 8 ounces of butter with a potent teaspoonful.

Water Bath Extraction

Step 1. In a large pot, preferably not aluminum, bring several quarts of water to a boil, then reduce the heat to a low simmer. Heating water this way produces a more even temperature throughout.

Step 2. Add your marijuana to the water—seeds, stems, shake, and all. Just dump it in, and disperse it by stirring, using a wooden spoon if you have one. Don't worry about the floaters.

Step 3. Cover the pot and simmer the marijuana on low heat for about two hours. Water temperature should be hot to the touch but nowhere near a boil. Stir the marijuana every so often.

Step 4. After two hours of gently simmering the marijuana in water alone, add the butter by dropping it into the pot. See the previous section for how much butter to add. It's best to use pasteurized butter, but you don't have to. You may also want to clarify your butter first (see p. 122).

Step 5. The butter will melt within minutes after being added, and you should stir the contents of the pot frequently over the next two hours. Keep the pot covered except when you're stirring. If the water level drops, replenish it with hot tap water.

Step 6. When you're ready to take the pot off, after a total cooking time of four hours (two hours simmering with only water, two hours simmering with butter added), heat a small kettle of water to boiling on the side.

Step 7. Make ready a bowl, a strainer through which you'll pour the liquid and catch all the marijuana, and several pot holders.

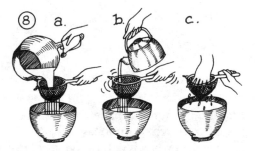

Step 8. Pour the marijuana/butter liquid through the strainer into the bowl. Then slowly trickle the boiling water through the marijuana in the strainer, shaking the strainer as you pour. This removes all the butter clinging to the marijuana. Press the marijuana in the strainer to squeeze out the last of the liquid.

Step 9. Now you can discard the marijuana in the strainer; all its potency has been converted and transferred to the butter. If you're concerned about this, you can add fresh water to the pot, bring it to a simmer, and simmer the marijuana again for another two hours with a half stick of butter. This butter is rarely very potent, but it does act as a safeguard against tossing out marijuana with any potency remaining.

Step 10. Set aside the liquid to cool, keeping it covered. When the liquid has cooled several hours, put it into the refrigerator and chill it overnight.

Step 11. After complete cooling, the mixture will have separated into two or three layers.

The upper layer will be hard. It can be broken into large pieces and removed. It's easiest to slip a table knife under the hardened butter at the side of the bowl, pry it up, and break it into pieces.

The second layer will have a creamy, semisolid texture. It should be removed carefully with a large spoon. Care is necessary because you don't want to stir up the liquid below and lose some of the second layer by remixing it with the liquid.

The third layer is the liquid, mostly water and dissolved plant sugars, pigments, etc., but containing enough semi-emulsified butter particles to make it potent enough to keep. Use it to make sauces, to cook noodles, or whenever the taste and color will add to, not detract from, the appeal of a dish.

Step 12.   There is very little difference between the potency of the top two layers, so most people mix them together into a paste, which is then ready for marijuana food cookery. The creamy layer is a bit lighter in color and taste than the top layer, and is useful in delicate dishes. If you are making a dish calling for potency but not the herbal taste, you might want to set aside the creamy layer.

Step 13.   You should freeze the butter you aren't going to use immediately—but we'll explain storage in a while. Of course, you may not want to wait to cook with the butter. If that's how you feel, there's no reason not to try some buttered toast just as soon as you've completed your first batch of extract. From there, you can go in any cooking direction you want, from the very basic to the advanced and complex.

Alcohol Bath

Water bath extraction is the cheapest way to produce natural marijuana extracts for cooking, but using alcohol instead of water as the bath has many advantages, even if it does cost a little more per portion. This method is more efficient than the water bath because alcohol is a very effective solvent for the resin and THC molecules. Water, on the other hand, is totally ineffective as a solvent, and merely provides an environment of moist, nondestructive heat and a melting medium for the butter which absorbs the THC. In an alcohol bath, the THC molecules are first liberated and absorbed by the alcohol. The alcohol then cooks almost entirely away and passes the active THC over to the butter, which absorbs it completely. As the alcohol gradually evaporates, the THC becomes increasingly concentrated in the butter.

Alcohol bath butter extract of fresh marijuana, or marijuana with significant amounts of chlorophyll, is a brighter green than water bath extract, and has a more pronounced smell. The alcohol bath produces a more potent butter extract, and so is quite cost-effective as a method. You can use any high-proof alcohol you choose as the bath—rum and vodka work well. Rum baths have little effect on the taste of the butter, so if you want rum-flavored butter, first make the extract, then follow the flavoring procedures explained on p. 92.

You can use alcohol bath butter extract in any recipe where you don't mind the green color and taste, or where the taste can be effectively disguised.

Step 1. In alcohol bath extraction, you must heat ingredients in a double boiler over an electric stove or hotplate. Never heat alcohol directly on an electric burner, and, for God's sake, don't ever heat it on a gas burner. As the alcohol heats it produces explosive fumes, so work in a well-ventilated area. Heat water in the bottom of a double boiler to a low simmer over an electric stove or hotplate.

Step 2. Crush your marijuana and add 1 cup of alcohol for each ounce of marijuana to the top part of the double boiler.

Step 3. As soon as the alcohol is warm, add 8 ounces (two sticks) of butter for each ounce of marijuana soaking in the alcohol.

Step 4. Continue cooking, covered, for several hours, keeping enough water in the bottom of the double boiler at a low simmer. You may need to add a little alcohol, too, but toward the end of the cooking period, allow most of it to evaporate.

Step 5. Pour the emerald green liquid and the marijuana through a strainer into a bowl, and press the marijuana hard into the mesh to drain off the liquid.

Step 6. Heat a cup of alcohol in a double boiler, and, over a fresh bowl, pour it through the marijuana to remove the last of the butter. (If you don't do this over a fresh bowl, the alcohol will keep the butter from hardening thoroughly.)

Step 7. Let the two mixtures cool separately, covered, and chill overnight in the refrigerator.

Step 8. Skim off the congealed butter you extracted in Step 6 and add it to the bowl of now-hardened green marijuana butter. You can either refrigerate or freeze this butter. The alcohol you used to extract the last of the butter can be set aside for later use in a sauce.

Microwave Magic

If you have a microwave oven you're in luck (in some ways, at least) because you have a much simpler method of making marijuana extracts at your disposal.

Set your microwave on 50-percent power, place the marijuana on appropriate dishes, and cook the marijuana for 2½ minutes. Then, having melted the appropriate amount of butter in the top of a double boiler, add the cooked marijuana.

The microwave time has converted a high proportion of inactive THC to active form, and so all that is needed is for the butter to absorb the already converted THC. Thus, cooking time is radically decreased, and after 30 minutes, the marijuana butter or bacon drippings or your choice of extract will be ready.

If, despite all the tempting recipes in this book you remain an incorrigible smoker, you too can benefit from microwave marijuana processing. Although smoking incinerates most of the THC, what does come over to the smoker is almost doubled in strength by the quick heating it has received in the microwave.

Storing Marijuana Extracts

The best approach is to make only the amount of extract you will be cooking with, just before you are ready to start cooking. However, it is definitely more convenient to have the extract already prepared. The choice is yours. If you choose the convenient route, you are going to have to store your extract. Marijuana butter, marijuana lard and marijuana bacon drippings (pp. 87–91) freeze very well. The best way is to mash the extract into a plastic ice cube tray, wrap the tray tightly in plastic, and seal it in an airtight bag after squeezing all the air out of the bag. If you're storing the extract for more than three weeks, use freezer wrap.

Most plastic ice cube trays have compartments which make little cubes measuring about ¼ cup in volume, which is a very convenient amount to be able to have on hand when you want it. If your recipe calls for ½ cup of marijuana butter, simply pop two cubes out of the tray, reseal it, and proceed. (You may want to take the amount of extract you'll use out of the freezer to thaw and soften a couple of hours before you start to cook.)

The three principal dangers to marijuana potency are, in order of seriousness, light, air, and moisture. When preparing extracts, keeping the lid on the cooking vessel will minimize exposure to these three factors, and really does make a difference. The container used to store the extract should, ideally, keep light and air out, and prevent any moisture exchange. Tupperware makes a wide variety of suitable containers, or a coffee can with a tight plastic lid will do as well. If stored in the freezer in airtight containers, most extracts will last quite well up to four months. Bacon drippings will keep forever.

You freeze butter, lard, and bacon drippings, also any semivegetarian butter and oil combinations, if they are not going to be used right away. Heavy cream extract should be used immediately, and so should other extract bases not covered here, including yogurt, true sour cream, the soft, meltable cheeses, and cocoa butter. These bases have limited use.

The basic directions for extract preparation apply to them as well.

The Trouble with Color

If there is a problem with butter extract, it's the color. Depending on the marijuana used, the butter can range in color from bright green to dark green to yellow to brown. In some dishes color is important, and for these you should set aside light-colored but potent butter in ideal freezer storage conditions.

If you are fortunate enough to have some very fine well-cured buds, you can produce a very light colored, aromatic, potent butter extract to use in the more delicate dishes. Other dishes, such as casseroles, baked goods, and sauces, allow you to disguise a brilliant-, dark- or bilious-colored marijuana butter with the color and flavors of other ingredients. In such dishes, it's not so much the color as the taste that's important. Fortunately, you can usually control the flavor (see pp. 92–95).

CHAPTER *7*

Variations on a Theme

Now that you've got the basics down, you're ready to move on to the various extraction processes we've devised for special kinds of marijuana and special cooking situations. These next few pages reveal the secrets of making extract from marijuana seedlings, from the very finest flowering tops as well as the very worst kind of weed. And once you've learned how to make marijuana extract with lard, cream, bacon drippings and olive oil, you'll be ready and able to tailor your marijuana cooking or baking to meet any festive occasion.

Small Batches of Butter Extract

Now let's imagine you are the sole proprietor of some flowering tops, perhaps a warm, silky cluster weighing 7 grams. The aroma of flowers and hot mint shimmers in your nose.

To extract a small amount of fine marijuana, let's say just two or three buds, with a small amount of butter or other extract base, proceed as follows.

Step 1. In the top of a double boiler, melt whatever amount of butter you've decided to use. The water below need only be at a slow simmer. Clarified butter will preserve fine marijuana taste better than unclarified butter (see p. 122 for instructions on clarifying).

Step 2. When the butter has melted, bruise and separate the marijuana but don't crumble it, and drop it in the butter.

Step 3. If the marijuana isn't covered by the butter, you can (a) add more butter, (b) turn the marijuana frequently, or (c) add some vodka, rum, brandy, or your choice of alcohol (stay away from grain for the process).

Step 4. Heat the marijuana butter for two hours, stirring frequently. If using alcohol, allow it to evaporate; otherwise, keep the pot covered. Check to be sure the water below isn't boiling away.

Step 5. After two hours, pour the melted butter into a crock, cover the crock, and allow it to cool thoroughly. Whether you want to filter out the marijuana pieces or not is optional. We sometimes like to strain the butter as we pour it off, trapping seeds and shake. Then, carefully removing as many seeds as possible from the buds, we put the buds back into the butter and allow the butter to solidify around them. When the butter is finally used, the buds are recovered intact from the center of the butter. During their time in cold storage, they have imparted a wonderful flavor, aroma, and intensity to the butter immediately around them. A piece of bud 'n' butter (God—can't you see the signs), the size of a small fingernail, dropped into a hot rum drink or a cup of espresso will send wonderful little shivers through your toes and ears.

Extract from Low-Grade Marijuana

Well, all right, it's nice if you have wonderful buds and can make fantastic butter that gets you off in a tiny cup, but what about reality? Until everyone is free to grow top-grade personal marijuana, there's going to be a lot of bad commercial shit bought, a lot of furtive, light-deprived marijuana grown.

Let's talk about all that bad stuff. All it takes to turn lead into gold is to refine matters, and concentrate.

Step 1. Determine just how bad this stuff is. Are you sure it's marijuana? Don't laugh—there's a lot of jimsonweed around, and jimsonweed butter will surely kill you. If you've got a lid you think is anything but marijuana, please just toss it. A lid of cheap street grass that has no seeds and is completely "manicured" should be distrusted.

Step 2. Anyhow, if you have *really* bad marijuana, you will want to get a big kettle of water ready. Bring it to a boil, then lower it to a simmer. Add your marijuana. Allow it to simmer for two hours, stirring frequently.

Step 3. After two hours, drop in 1 or 2 ounces of butter for every 4 ounces of marijuana—a stick or two of butter a pound, depending on just how bad you think your stuff is. One stick per pound is for rope-quality hemp, stuff so weak it's impossible to get off by smoking it.

Step 4. Continue simmering the mixture for two more hours. No doubt you will begin to see shapes in the steam, and black cats will appear at your window expectantly. Resist the urge to cackle, and be cool. As soon as four hours total have elapsed, remove the brew from the heat.

Step 5. Pour off the liquid through a strainer into a pot. Then pour boiling water through the material in the strainer to get the last of the butter out. Squeeze the material thoroughly, then toss the weed onto the compost heap—it had little to begin with, but now it has nada, rien, zilch, and there's nothing left to do but to return it as quickly as possible to earth.

Step 6. The butter, on the other hand, will congeal as always on the top of the cooled water. There won't be a lot of it, and it may be an ugly color, and it will definitely smell pungent, but watch out! It'll getcha.

Step 7. Still watching out, you now have to test the butter. Try a teaspoon on a piece of toast, sit back, and prepare to evaluate the high your butter produces. First, after an hour, ask yourself the question "Am I high?" If the answer is "Am I high!" then you know your alchemical sorcery has succeeded, and you've indeed turned lead into gold: If, instead, you answer, "No, but I've got an awful headache," then your weed was unsalvageable anyway, and you're better off taking a few aspirin and throwing the butter out. In either case, let's leave the depressing subject of the marginal weed and go on to a completely new approach to coping with inflation, specifically, the cost of getting high index.

Seedling Butter Extract

Let's say you have just purchased a pound of seedy Colombian Gold. If you are very lucky, the raunchy stuff will be only about one-third seeds, which of course we are all accustomed to treating as useless. They can be planted, naturally, but unless you are into big-time farming, you won't really have any use for most of the seeds, and they will have to be thrown away.

Not so! Using a very simple procedure, anyone can realize double their investment from a pound of street marijuana. Here's how.

If you're planting indoors, simply use a deep cookie sheet or an aluminum-foil pan or any other container that will allow you a planting medium about 2 inches deep, using a mixture of 75 percent soil and 25 percent pumice or vermiculite. If you're planting outdoors, simply spade up a patch of likely earth and work in a little pumice for aeration of the soil. Plant the seeds about ¼ inch deep, and no more than an inch or so apart. This means that in an area 18 by 24 inches you will have plus or minus 400 seeds planted.

Tend the seedlings by watering them only lightly and making sure there is adequate light. It will help if the environment is warm. If you are planting indoors, you may want to make sure that the trays are located in an evenly heated area —near a radiator, for example. Or the trays can be warmed from below with an incandescent bulb.

You are going to raise the little marijuana plants until they are about 21 days old, then harvest them and dry them. At three weeks, it will take around 75 to 100 seedlings to make ½ ounce of dry marijuana, so each cookie sheet should yield between 2 and 3 ounces of dried marijuana when harvested.

Marijuana seedling potency is not well understood. We all know that some seedlings are very potent, and some are so mild they might as well be parsley. But if you take three-week-old marijuana seedlings and use them to make butter extract, you will wind up with butter as potent as any you have ever made, provided you have a fairly high ratio of seedling material to butter. I've found that if I extract 4 ounces of dried three-week seedlings with 6 ounces of butter I get a very nice, very strong extract which has a wonderful fresh flavor impossible to achieve with most mature plants.

And best of all, this butter is a true bonus! From the seeds in a pound of average Colombian marijuana, you should be able to make a pound or more of dried seedlings after sprouting them all. These seedlings in turn translate into 1½ pounds butter, or roughly 150 teaspoons butter, which you would not have had if you hadn't used the sprout-and-extract technique.

This bonus butter can be used many ways. You can bake marijuana cookies and sell them to offset the price of the original purchase. You can use some to make gifts for friends. You can consume some in whatever way gives you pleasure. But however you choose to use the bonus seedlings, you'll find that by using this technique, even the exorbitant price of good street marijuana can be brought within reason when measured in cost-per-dose terms.

Marijuana Butter Sauté

As we sail down the seas of butter and hemp, we come to the straits of sauté. Fellow marijuana mariners, these are great straits, because if you aren't careful you can burn your buds and lose your potency. Still, an approach to sautéing is worth having on your charts.

Butter made potent by a brief sautéing with marijuana buds can be used, in turn, to sauté other foods in other dishes. This procedure is useful when you only want to make a small amount of marijuana butter on the spot for a stovetop recipe.

Step 1. Remove loose seeds from your stash of buds, using about 5 grams of fairly clean buds to one stick of butter.

Step 2. Use a cast-iron skillet, or cooking pottery if possible. Melt the butter very slowly over low heat. You want a setting that melts the butter but never browns the edges of the melted butter.

Step 3. Drop the semicleaned marijuana buds into the melted butter, and then raise the heat just a bit. Stirring the contents of the pan with a wooden implement if possible (metal utensils tend to break up whatever you're cooking), add a little butter every few minutes to top off the pan butter. Sauté gently for 20 minutes, then remove the pan from the heat.

Step 4. Actually, a step aside, to tell you that this approach works extremely well with bacon drippings. Also, really interesting bacon and eggs can be created by taking fresh slab bacon and cooking the bacon and some good marijuana together very slowly for 20 minutes. Some of the THC is converted and absorbed by the fat remaining in the bacon. Some is absorbed by the drippings that you will pour off and keep for future gourmet highs. Some is present in the film of bacon fat left in the pan, which you can use to fry or scramble the eggs.

Pick the remaining buds out of the somewhat cooled bacon grease, and store them in the freezer in a closed jar. They still have potency left, but they're the world's greasiest smoke, so if any of your marauding friends spot them behind the ice cream, you're safe. However, they work wonders in refried beans (see recipe, p. 129).

So, Step 5.   Back to butter. You've sautéed your buds, so pour off the butter through a strainer. Then, reserving the buds for storage, go right ahead with a recipe that calls for the use of butter for sautéing.

Lard Extract

Lard is extraordinarily useful in marijuana food preparation. It is a key ingredient in some very potent pastries and crusts, and makes many wonderful sauces and basting mixtures. It is a very efficient vehicle for absorption of the potency of marijuana.

Since lard is used sparingly in most recipes, it's best to make only very potent lard, and to watch extract-per-portion calculations carefully (see p. 103 on calculating dosage). For moderate-to-mediocre marijuana, use 4 ounces of marijuana to 1 pound of lard, or 1 ounce of marijuana to 4 ounces of lard, to yield approximately 24 teaspoons of very potent lard.

To prepare marijuana lard, follow these simple steps.

Step 1.   In a large pot, bring 4 quarts of water to a boil, then reduce to simmer.

Step 2.   Add 4 ounces of marijuana—everything, including stems. If you are lucky or foresighted enough to have some nice homegrown sinsemilla and have plenty, then use just tops, but watch out for potency. Consider reducing the amount of marijuana by half with potent sinsemilla.

Step 3. Cover the pot, and simmer the marijuana at low heat for two hours. Water temperature should be hot to the touch, around 120°. Stir the marijuana occasionally, with a wooden spoon if possible. Add water if necessary.

Step 4. Bring a pan of water to a boil, using 1 quart of water in a 4-quart pot. Add the lard. Boil until the lard is thoroughly melted, then pour immediately into the pot with the simmering marijuana.

Step 5. Cover the pot and continue to simmer, stirring well every 15 minutes.

Step 6. When you are ready to take the pot off after another two hours for a total cooking time of four hours (a little more or less doesn't hurt or change anything), put a kettle of water on to boil.

Step 7. Make ready a large heatproof container, a fine-mesh strainer, and several good pot holders.

Step 8. Pour the contents of the marijuana/lard pot slowly through the strainer into the large heatproof container. When that is done, slowly trickle the boiling water you have ready through the marijuana in the strainer, to remove the last of the trapped lard.

Step 9. Use the marijuana left in the strainer for compost or throw it away or set it out to be picked over by hungry birds as their last resort in hard times—it's no good to you any-more. All the goodies have been transferred to the lard, which is now beginning to congeal on top of the water in the pot as it cools.

Step 10. After several hours of cooling, take the top layer of lard off with a spoon, and put it into the fridge in a covered jar. Wait several hours and skim again, keeping all the skimmed lard in the fridge. Set the pot out overnight to cool completely, and in the morning skim off the last of the lard. The water is now useless, unlike the water used in making marijuana butter. At least, nobody we know has yet found a use for lard water. If you do, please let us know.

Step 11. The lard freezes very well, and, in our experience, keeps for up to six months under simple refrigeration. It flavors easily with fresh herbs and a variety of other flavor-ings. Be sure to label the lard clearly in your freezer, and it's not a bad idea to date it, either.

Bacon Drippings Extract

Bacon drippings extract can be prepared in a number of ways for marijuana food cooking. A very convenient method is the water bath extraction technique used for butter (see p. 73). You simply use 1 cup of bacon drippings to 1 ounce of ordinary marijuana, simmering the marijuana for two hours in water before adding the bacon drippings to the water, continuing to simmer for two hours more. Pour off the liquid, pour boiling water through the marijuana in the strainer, set the liquid aside to cool, chill overnight, and remove the now-potent congealed drippings with a spoon.

With very potent marijuana, which requires only a few grams of flowering tops to ½ cup or so of extract base, you can use a double boiler as you would with butter.

With bacon drippings you can also sauté intact flower heads over very low heat for about 20 to 30 minutes in a cast-iron saucepan. These sautéed tops make wonderfully crunchy refried black beans, or are great by themselves with a little salsa. Whatever your gustatory scheme for bacon drippings, keep in mind that they are going to taste like bacon no matter how you prepare them.

Heavy Cream Extract

Heavy cream extraction requires the use of a double boiler. For this reason you will have to use a small amount of pretty good marijuana, since you want to be able to cover the marijuana without having to use large amounts of cream. Again, sinsemilla buds are the ideal form of the herb for heavy cream extraction. Keep the water below at a steady, gentle boil, and stir the cream/marijuana mixture in the top frequently. Use only heavy cream which is pasteurized, and buy the freshest cream possible. Many grocery stores put the freshest dairy products in the back of the case, and those with the shortest remaining life in the front—so it pays to check the date on the carton.

Cook the cream, covered, for about 1½ hours, then strain, and allow the liquid to cool. The skim on the top should not be thrown away, since it's as potent as the rest. You should not pour boiling water through the marijuana in the strainer into the cream, but you can make a small amount of tea out of the marijuana in a separate cup, and get a very nice cup of high for yourself, and several other people no doubt.

Semivegetarian Extract

I'm sure some people would prefer a more vegetarian approach to marijuana food. While we haven't been able to discover an effective purely vegetarian approach, there are modified approaches which work quite well. The best, most versatile one we've come up with is olive butter extract.

Begin by making potent butter extract as usual. Then, instead of pouring water through the marijuana remaining in the strainer, heat about 1½ cups of good olive oil in a small saucepan until it's very hot, just before it begins to boil. Pour this hot olive oil through the marijuana in the strainer into a jar or pan of its own.

Put the olive oil and marijuana butter aside to cool, then refrigerate overnight. When both have solidified nicely, take off the marijuana butter—both layers—and blend with the solidified olive oil. You will now have a mixture which will keep in the refrigerator or freezer, which will not separate, which can be used in a vast number of pasta dishes, casseroles, omelettes, or whatever you wish, which contains a minimal amount of animal fat, and which we feel represents a nice compromise between pure vegetarian considerations and the acknowledged dangers of smoking as opposed to eating marijuana. You can follow the same procedures using grapeseed oil and get good results.

Flavoring the Extract

A cook who is preparing marijuana extract with fine homegrown, minty, potent sinsemilla will have no problem deciding on the taste blend of the food—it will have marijuana as a principal theme. However, when a cook is faced with ¼ pound of very potent barnyard Colombian, which, if not handled properly, will result in a marijuana butter that makes everything it's used in taste either like old wet books or stale underwear, the question arises—just how do you cover that rotting rug smell and flavor, anyhow?

It ain't easy, partner, but it usually can be done.

I make my own flavoring agents for marijuana extracts from a variety of herbs, spices, and even fruits, using either an alcohol or water base. The instructions for making water or alcohol extracts are given below, and a list of flavoring agents follow, specifying which base to use for each herb or spice.

To make an alcohol base flavoring extract, use a double boiler, again heating only on an electric stove to avoid the danger from explosive fumes. Prepare the herb or spice you are going to extract (e.g., bruise the flowers, crush the clove lightly, grind the nutmeg). The amount of material you use will determine the extract strength. Place the material in the top of the double boiler, cover with alcohol, and bring the water in the bottom of the double boiler to a low boil. Usually, 30 minutes of simmering will produce an excellent extract. Filter the extracts, where indicated, by pouring through a paper coffee filter into a container. These filters are strong and cheap.

We've found that inexpensive vodka makes an excellent base. You can also use rum, port, sherry, or any other strong drink as the alcohol base.

You can make a cold alcohol extract simply by soaking the flavoring herb in the proper amount of alcohol for one to three weeks, then filtering.

Water base extract is generally weaker than alcohol base extract. To make water base extract, you need a single pot. You're basically just making tea. Again, prepare the herb or spice by bruising, grinding, or crushing, heat for 1 to 1½ hours, and filter. Don't try to make extract by soaking in cold water; it doesn't work.

Rose Alcohol or warm water extract, petals only; use ⅔ cup unpacked petals to 1½ cups alcohol or 2 cups water. Simmer 60 minutes, then strain. You may want to clip the little white base, or hip, off the petals to reduce bitterness and enhance the rose flavor.

Vanilla Make your own, using alcohol and a vanilla bean, one bean to ½ pint alcohol. Simmer 30 minutes, then filter. Mexican beans have an excellent flavor. If you're making cold extract, vanilla beans can soak practically forever.

Anise Alcohol extract of the bruised seed, 1½ teaspoons seed to 1 cup alcohol. Simmer 20 to 30 minutes, then filter. Bruise the seed on wax paper over a hard surface by running a rolling pin back and forth over it, pressing fairly hard but not crushing the seed. For cold extract, soak bruised seeds two weeks.

Orange Alcohol extract of lightly crushed orange peel, peel of half an orange to 1 cup alcohol. Simmer 15 to 20 minutes, then remove the peel. To crush the peel, twist and pinch it between your fingers. For cold extract, soak one week and remove the peel.

Cassia Alcohol extract of the chopped root, 1 teaspoon very finely chopped root to ½ cup alcohol. Simmer 45 minutes, then filter. Don't extract cold.

Clove Alcohol extract of lightly crushed cloves, four cloves to 1 cup alcohol. Crush cloves with a rolling pin on wax paper. Simmer 20 to 30 minutes, then filter. For a strong cold extract, crush cloves, soak two weeks, then remove the cloves.

Mace Alcohol extract of grated mace, ½ teaspoon grated mace to 1 cup alcohol. Simmer 20 minutes, then filter. For cold extract, soak one week, then filter well.

Nutmeg 1 teaspoon freshly ground nutmeg to ½ cup alcohol. Simmer 30 minutes, then filter. For cold extract, soak one week, then filter.

Cinnamon 1 teaspoon to ½ cup alcohol. Simmer 30 minutes, then filter well. For cold extract, soak one week, then filter.

Caraway 1 teaspoon crushed seed to 1 cup alcohol. Simmer 20 minutes, then filter.

Sassafras 1 tablespoon dry leaves crushed in 1 cup alcohol. Simmer 30 minutes, then filter. The leaves are available under the name "gumbo filé."

Juniper Four to six berries, fresh or dry, to 1 cup alcohol. Simmer 30 minutes over very low heat, then filter. For cold extract, soak lightly bruised berries three weeks.

Lemon Peel of ½ lemon, bruised, to 1 cup alcohol. Follow directions for orange.

Pennyroyal ¼ cup fresh flowers, bruised, to 1 cup alcohol. Simmer 10 minutes, then filter. For cold extract, soak three weeks.

Rosemary 1 tablespoon fresh, bruised rosemary to 1 cup alcohol. Simmer 20 minutes, then filter. For cold extract, soak three weeks.

Coriander or Cilantro Alcohol extract of a few crushed fresh flowers, four fresh leaves to ½ cup alcohol. Simmer 20 to 25 minutes, then filter. Cilantro flavor on tobacco needs a sweetener. For cold extract, soak one week, then filter.

Geranium Alcohol extract of whole fresh flowers, ½ cup flowers to ¾ cup alcohol. Simmer 10 to 15 minutes, then filter.

Lavender Alcohol extract of bruised flower petals only, ½ cup petals to 1 cup alcohol. Simmer 10 to 15 minutes, then filter.

Chamomile Alcohol extract of bruised whole flowers, ½ cup packed flowers to 1 cup alcohol. Simmer 20 to 30 minutes, then filter.

Flavoring marijuana extracts will take a little experimenting on your part, since the kinds and amounts of flavorings needed will depend on the marijuana you are using and your own tastes and preferences. First divide ¼ pound of marijuana into a keeper pile of about 3 ounces and an experimental pile of an ounce or a little less. *None* of the nice buds should go into the experimental pile; in fact, the more sticks, seeds, and shit you can use to experiment with the better, because a sack of that raunchy Colombian stuff all smells and tastes alike anyway, and why use any of the best part to test for flavor?

Take a whiff of the marijuana you're trying to blend, cover, or make go away, and try to imagine how one or a combination of the above flavors will blend with it. Once you've decided on your flavoring (or combination of flavorings), make up a miniature recipe using the ounce of marijuana and 8 ounces of butter. You'll probably want to start with a teaspoon or so of flavoring extract, but if this doesn't turn out to do the trick, add more until you're satisfied with the taste of your marijuana butter extract.

For the flavoring agents which depend on volatile oils for their effect, such as fresh herbs, it's best to wait until well into the fat absorption process to add the flavoring agent. We feel that if you add it 15 to 20 minutes before you are about to take the extract off the stove, the fat in the liquid will pick up most of the flavor you want. If you are using a flavoring agent which is nonvolatile, such as coffee, you can successfully add it any time during the last hour of cooking. If you are dealing with flavoring agents which evaporate easily, such as vanilla extract, you may want to wait until the marijuana extract has been removed from the heat and is in the process of cooling.

As you can see, there are no firm rules to follow in flavoring marijuana extracts. You will find, however, that the raunchier the marijuana you are dealing with, the more flavoring you will have to add and the earlier in the cooking process you are going to want to start the flavoring process. If you are using volatile flavoring agents, this may mean that you will have to add the flavors several times during the course of cooking.

When you've got your solidified extract, do a little taste test, either by spreading a little marijuana butter on toast or by using the experimental batch in a test recipe. Once you've arrived at amounts of flavoring agents that work well, memorize the number of teaspoons you use per cup of marijuana extract, and keep that ratio constant in future batches of extract. For example, if you use 1 teaspoon of flavoring per cup of marijuana butter made with 1 ounce of marijuana and 8 ounces of butter, use 2 teaspoons in 1-pound batches of extract, and so on.

Be open to experimentation, using principally the trashy part of your marijuana, as I said, and don't forget, even the failures in your flavor experiments are potent, so don't throw them out.

PART III

Cooking with Marijuana Extracts

CHAPTER 8

Recipes for the High Diner

You can use marijuana extract in almost any recipe calling for the straight version, but, obviously, different batches of extract prepared from different plants by different folks are going to be different.

The recipes that follow have all been tested, and highly approved, by a number of people, but that doesn't mean that we've got a definitive cookbook going here. Many of the recipes are for goodies—which is as it should be, since getting high is largely a matter of fun, and goodies seem a nice way to get there. There are also a few more "serious" recipes and ideas, since the art of cooking, and the art of being high, can be pursued on many different levels.

Eating to get high as part of the pleasure opens up new areas of gourmet appreciation of food and its psychic role. Getting high through the belly chakra is a far more profound experience than getting high through the throat and chest chakras, and the impact of earth and water in food far more nurturing than the impact of fire and smoke. Since the membranes of the mouth are very efficient absorbers of THC, it is an exercise in contemplation to chew marijuana food slowly, with attention, and to feel the initial hint of high coming through the brain direct from the food in the mouth.

At the top of each recipe you'll find information on the number of portions involved, and a rough gauge of the potency of each recipe. Extracts will vary in potency, of course, but even more varied will be individual response to a portion of marijuana food. So much depends on how much you eat, whether or not anything else is eaten too, when you last ate, how your health is, whether you have any allergic reaction, what other drugs you may have been using, etc.—there are just too many individual factors at work to make any accurate general statement about how potent each recipe is.

So—do go slow, okay? This recipe section is intended as a guide, a starting point from which you can carve out your individual experience with marijuana food.

The most notable statement that can be made about the
vast majority of marijuana users, experimenters, and inter-
mittent users, is that they are essentially indistinguishable
from their non-marijuana-using peers by any fundamental
criterion other than marijuana use.

—Schaeffer Commission on
Marijuana and Drug Abuse

Well, the commission is almost right. Actually, marijuana
fiends do vary slightly from their non-marijuana using peers
on one fundamental count: goodie consumption. In that
most basic of human behavior patterns—the urge to gorge
lying right next to the urge to merge in the center of the
human psyche—it's fair to say that cannabis lovers are ab-
normal. The Cookie Monster on Sesame Street has a mild
cookie fixation compared with the deep drives developed by
someone who is really hammered-out on THC.

Now let's talk about using the extracts for a good, safe
high.

Calculating Extract Dosage

Many people make the mistake of overdoing marijuana
butter once, but that usually doesn't happen again. The
physiological aspects of eating marijuana are covered in another place. The point to be made here is that you should
start with a maximum of 1 teaspoon of whatever 8:1 ratio
extract you make, and for God's sake, *give it time*. The problem is that it takes a while to reach the high through eating,
so many folks will take that first cookie or slice of quiche or
omelette with a teaspoon of extract in it, wait an hour, and
think nothing's happening. So maybe they take another
cookie, or Lord help them, a couple of cookies. They figure
that will probably do the trick. Well, it certainly will. Anyone
taking the approach that if one is good, two is better, ought
to be *real* near someplace very comfortable to lie down, and
have nothing to do for the next half day or so.

The point on dosage is GO SLOW. If you are a person who

gets high pretty easily, you will want to begin with a small amount of extract, say ¼ teaspoon. If you have used a lower base to marijuana ratio, say, 1 pound of butter to 4 ounces of marijuana, then reduce the amount of extract proportionately. There are times when the lower ratio is advantageous, for instance, when you are extracting some particularly fine sinsemilla and want a concentrated hit of that sweet, minty flavor.

When you are cooking with marijuana extract, it's pretty simple to calculate dosage in relation to portion size. Let's say you want to make some chocolate chip cookies. The classic recipe on the back of many chocolate chip packages calls for ½ cup of butter to one pack of chips, and the recipe makes about 4 dozen cookies. Since you know that ½ cup (4 ounces) of marijuana butter will yield 8 tablespoons, or 24 teaspoons of butter, it's clear that each cookie will contain ½ teaspoon of butter. This means that two cookies will give you the equivalent of 1 teaspoon's potency. Now, if you are a real cookie freak and just can't possibly get by without eating a bunch of cookies at a time, you'll want to cut down on the potency per cookie—I hope. To do that is easy. Simply use, say, ¼ cup of marijuana butter and ¼ cup of regular butter in the recipe, and you will have cut the potency to ¼ teaspoon's worth per cookie, giving you the freedom to eat four cookies instead of two. If you want to reduce the potency per cookie even more, so that you can eat more at a sitting, simply cut the ratio of potent butter to straight butter even lower. And, of course, you'll want to make sure that the cookies are uniform in size and that you do get the full 48 cookies out of the recipe.

But now let's say that there are young children in your home, and you figure it's dangerous to have a batch of potent cookies around. Remembering our own childhoods, we realize the futility of trying to hide anything resembling a treat or a secret anywhere in the house. Don't worry. As we've pointed out elsewhere, there is no limit to what you can cook once you have prepared marijuana extracts properly. For instance, one of my favorite personal antichild marijuana foods is Cannabis quiche Lorraine. We'll get to the recipe later on, but for now let's just agree, if we can, that quiche is not exactly a universal favorite among kids. Let's say that you have used ¼ cup of marijuana butter in your 12-inch quiche, an amount which means that there will be about 12 teaspoons of marijuana butter dispersed throughout the quiche. This means that if you are having a dozen friends over for the evening, you can start each of them off (or finish them off!) with a small slice of your killer quiche as an opener, and count on the entire mob being nicely high by the time dinner actually rolls around.

Incidentally, when you are serving marijuana food to friends at a party, you'll find that instead of being stuck with an enormous bill for wine, beer, and booze at the end of the evening, your party will go just as well if you serve only juices and teas for drinks, because once a person is nicely high on marijuana food, sloshing down a lot of alcohol is not only redundant, it gets in the way of enjoying the marijuana high. A plus, of course, is that there is no hangover the next morning.

I hope that by now the principles of calculating dosage per portion is clear. It's pretty simple, so let me run through it quickly step by step: First, calculate how many portions you want from whatever recipe you're using, then figure 1 teaspoon per portion, or ½ teaspoon per portion if that's how you want to do it. Next, figure the equivalent in cup measures: 12 teaspoons equals ¼ cup, 24 teaspoons equals ½ cup, 36 teaspoons equals ¾ cup, 48 teaspoons equals 1 cup, and so on. If the recipe calls for, say, 1 cup of butter and yields only 12 portions, use ¼ cup of marijuana butter and ¾ cup of regular butter. Or, if the recipe calls for ½ cup butter and yields 24 portions, use all marijuana butter.

Sweets

Hence, fellow heads, begin the sweets section of this high endeavor with the most American of cookies—the chocolate chip.

Marijuana Chocolate Chip Cookies

YIELD: 48 cookies
POTENCY: ½ teaspoon per cookie

This recipe is classic and can be found on every bag of chocolate chips in the world.

½ cup marijuana butter
6 tablespoons brown sugar
6 tablespoons turbinado (unrefined) sugar
1 large egg
½ teaspoon vanilla extract
1 cup plus 2 tablespoons unbleached white flour
½ teaspoon sea salt
½ teaspoon baking soda
1 cup chocolate chips, or an equal amount of exotic semi-sweet chocolate broken into bean-sized pieces
½ cup chopped nuts

1. Cream the butter with the brown and white sugars until fluffy.
2. Beat in the egg and vanilla.
3. Sift the flour, sea salt, and baking soda together, and stir into the creamed mixture.
4. Stir in the chocolate chips and nuts.
5. Chill the cookie dough for at least two hours. (This is a precaution against the dreaded flat cookie: Chilled dough bakes vertically, not horizontally. But, if you like flat cookies, don't chill the dough.)
6. Lightly butter cookie sheets using marijuana butter. Drop the dough onto the prepared cookie sheets by teaspoonfuls 2 inches apart. Bake in a preheated 375° oven for eight minutes, or until as brown as you like them.

Oatmeal Sinsemilla Cookies

YIELD: 70 to 80 cookies
POTENCY: ½ teaspoon per cookie

Another great traveling treat, these cookies feature a nice combination of spices which effectively mask the odor of most marijuana butter, and they keep well.

      2 extra large eggs
     ¾ cup marijuana butter
      2 cups turbinado (unrefined) sugar
      2 teaspoons vanilla extract
      1 tablespoon ground nutmeg
      1 tablespoon ground cloves
      1 tablespoon ground cinnamon
      2 cups whole-wheat flour
     ½ teaspoon baking soda
      1 teaspoon sea salt
      2 tablespoons water
   1½ cups raisins
      2 cups rolled oats
      1 cup pecan pieces

1. Cream together the eggs, butter, sugar, and vanilla.
2. Sift together the spices, flour, soda, and salt, and add to the creamed mixture.
3. Add the water, raisins, oats, and pecans, and mix thoroughly.
4. Chill the dough.
5. Place spoon-sized chunks of dough on a buttered cookie sheet. If you wish, top with coarse sugar crystals.
6. Bake in a preheated 350° oven for 15 to 20 minutes.

Jam-Filled Ganja Crumbles

YIELD: 40 to 45 cookies
POTENCY: ¾ teaspoon per cookie

⅔ cup marijuana butter
¾ cup turbinado (unrefined) sugar
1 egg
1½ cups good-quality rolled oats
1 teaspoon sea salt
½ cup whole-wheat flour
1 teaspoon double-acting baking powder (aluminum free)
½ cup chopped pecans
1 cup strawberry, raspberry, or black-currant jam

1. Combine the butter and sugar in a large bowl.
2. Add the egg, oats, and salt. Mix well.
3. Combine and sift together the flour and baking powder, then add to the bowl. Stir in the pecans. Chill the dough 2 hours.
4. Drop by teaspoonfuls on a lightly buttered cookie sheet. Make a slight depression in each center with your thumb, and spoon in a bit of jam.
5. Bake for eight minutes in a preheated 350° oven. Allow to cool before removing from the cookie sheet.

Sinsemilla Orange Drops

YIELD: 36 cookies
POTENCY: ⅔ teaspoon per cookie

    2 large, fresh organic eggs
    ½ cup light, potent marijuana butter (Use some of your
       most aromatic for these light cookies.)
    ½ cup raw clover honey
    ½ teaspoon sea salt
    1¼ cups whole-wheat flour
    1 teaspoon double-acting baking powder (aluminum
       free)
    ½ teaspoon pumpkin pie spice, or equal parts ground
       cloves, cinnamon, nutmeg, and allspice
    2 tablespoons orange juice
    ½ cup grated orange rind (from a ripe organic orange)
    1 cup flaked oats
    ½ cup chopped hazelnuts

1. In a large bowl beat together the eggs, butter, honey, and
   salt.
2. Sift together the flour, baking powder, and pumpkin pie
   spice, and stir into the egg mixture.
3. Stir in the orange juice, orange rind, oats, and hazelnuts.
   Taste the batter and adjust the flavoring, if desired, by
   adding more salt, orange juice or rind. Chill the dough 2
   hours.
4. Drop by teaspoonfuls onto a lightly buttered cookie sheet.
   Bake in a preheated 350° oven for 10 to 12 minutes, or
   until crisp around the edges.

Blueberry Blastoffs

YIELD: 24 muffins
POTENCY: 1½ teaspoons per muffin

The taste of blueberries and fine sinsemilla butter combine in this recipe to provide all the potency you need to get that Sunday brunch off to a fast start and lazy finish.

⅔ cup marijuana butter
1 cup turbinado (unrefined) sugar
3 large, fresh eggs
2 teaspoons double-acting aluminum-free baking powder
1 teaspoon sea salt
3 cups twice-sifted all-purpose unbleached flour
1 cup whole milk
16 ounces frozen blueberries, thawed and drained

1. Cream the butter and sugar.
2. Beat the eggs, and mix them into the butter/sugar mixture.
3. Sift together the baking powder, salt, and flour. Add bit by bit to the mix, alternating with the milk. Don't overmix.
4. After the batter is mixed, gently fold in the blueberries.
5. Butter the muffin tins, and fill each cup two-thirds full. Bake in a preheated 375° oven for 30 minutes.

Jalapeño Gold Muffins

YIELD: 24 muffins
POTENCY: 1 teaspoon per muffin

½ cup marijuana butter
⅓ cup turbinado (unrefined) sugar
2 large fresh eggs
8 ounces creamed corn
1 cup sour cream
½ teaspoon sea salt
1 tablespoon aluminum-free baking powder
½ cup all-purpose, unbleached flour
1 cup grated sharp Cheddar cheese
¼ cup grated lemon peel
½ cup seeded, finely chopped Jalapeño peppers
1½ cups yellow corn meal

1. In a large bowl, cream together the butter, sugar, eggs, creamed corn, and sour cream.
2. Sift the salt, baking powder, and flour together and combine with the creamed mixture. Stir in the grated cheese, grated lemon, peppers, and corn meal. If necessary, adjust the taste with just a bit more sugar at a time.
3. Grease muffin tins with marijuana butter or any other shortening, and fill the cups two-thirds full. Bake in a preheated 450° oven for 18 to 20 minutes.

High Lime Pie

YIELD: 12 slices
POTENCY: 1 to 2 teaspoons per slice, depending on the ratio chosen for the pastry crust.

¼ cup water
1 package unflavored gelatin
1 cup sugar
½ tsp. salt
4 eggs, separated
½ cup lime juice, preferably Mexican limes, if available
2 teaspoons grated lime peel, plus 1 teaspoon for the topping
1 cup whipping cream
1 baked Rich Marijuana Pastry Crust (see p. 135)
Sweetened whipped cream
Lime slices
½ cup unsalted, shelled pistachio nuts

1. Combine the water and the gelatin. Allow to soften 5 minutes. Mix in half the sugar with the salt, egg yolks, and lime juice.
2. Stir constantly over medium heat until the mixture just begins to boil.
3. Remove the pan from the heat, and stir in 2 teaspoons of grated lime peel. (Add three drops of green food coloring at this point for a more pronounced color effect, if desired.)
4. Pour the mixture into a bowl and chill until slightly jelled.
5. Gradually add the remaining sugar to the cream, and whip until stiff peaks form. Fold into the chilled, somewhat jelled mixture.
6. Fill the pastry crust and chill the pie until the filling has firmly set.
7. Spread more sweetened whipped cream over the pie, place slices of fresh lime around the edge, and sprinkle the center with the pistachios and remaining lime peel.

Valencia Golden Goodies

YIELD: 40 to 48 pieces
POTENCY: ⅛ teaspoon per piece

This is a light-potency candy which makes a nice early evening treat along with a flowery white wine—sort of a garden-party high. You'll find a candy thermometer handy in working with this recipe. They only run about $10 and are a good tool to have around if you enjoy candy and want to create your own.

½ cup heavy cream
2 tablespoons potent marijuana butter
Grated peel from a firm, organic Valencia orange
2 cups turbinado (unrefined) sugar
1 cup light corn syrup
1 cup chopped pecans or almonds

1. In a large saucepan, combine the heavy cream, butter, orange peel, sugar, and corn syrup.
2. Cook the mixture, stirring continuously over medium-high heat, until the candy thermometer reaches 238°. *Or*, cook stirring constantly over medium-high heat until the mixture reaches the stage where a bit of it rolled between the thumb and index finger forms a soft ball in ice cold water.
3. Remove the pan from the heat, and stir in the nuts. Allow the mixture to cool somewhat.
4. Drop spoon-sized pieces onto a wax-paper-covered cookie sheet. Cool, put in a tight tin, and keep in a cool place.

Cannabis Caramel

YIELD: 100 pieces
POTENCY: ¼ teaspoon per piece

Look out! This is nearly irresistible. And the bonuses are that the candies keep for so long and travel very well without refrigeration. Be careful, though, to wrap each piece individually in wax paper, not in foil. Even better, if you'll be traveling with them, wrap them in the commercial wrappers from a tin of regular wrapped caramels. *Bon voyage!*

      2 cups turbinado (unrefined) sugar
     ½ teaspoon sea salt
      2 cups heavy cream
    1¾ cups light corn syrup
     ½ cup potent marijuana butter
      2 teaspoons vanilla extract
      1 teaspoon dark rum
      2 cups pecan pieces

1. In a large saucepan over medium-high heat, bring a mixture of the sugar, salt, 1 cup of the cream, corn syrup, and butter to a boil. Boil slowly for 10 minutes, stirring constantly. Do not scrape the bottom of the pan. (If you have buds left over which have been cooked but which have potency left, drop them in the mixture for the first 10 minutes, then remove them before proceeding.)
2. Dribble in the remaining cream, continuing to stir. Add the cream slowly enough not to disturb the boiling.
3. Continue to cook until a little of the mixture, when plopped into cold water and rolled between your thumb and index finger, forms a firm but not hard ball.
4. When the firm-ball stage is reached, remove the pan from the heat and stir in the vanilla, rum, and pecans. Pour out onto a buttered cookie sheet with sides, and allow to cool.
5. When the mix has cooled, cut into bite-sized pieces and wrap.

Quick High Pie

YIELD: 6 slices
POTENCY: 1½ teaspoons per slice

    25 chocolate wafer cookies
     3 tablespoons marijuana butter, softened
     1 pint mocha or coffee ice cream, softened
       Chocolate syrup

1. Crush the cookies into fine crumbs.
2. Reserve ½ cup crumbs and combine the butter with the remaining crumbs.
3. Using your fingers, spread the mixture evenly over the bottom and sides of a 9-inch pie pan.
4. Using another 9-inch pie pan, press down on the crumbs and butter to make a firm pie crust.
5. Spoon the softened ice cream into the prepared crust.
6. Top with the reserved crumbs, pour chocolate syrup over the top in swirls, and chill in the freezer.

Touch o' the Hemp Brownies

YIELD: 45 to 50 1½-inch squares
POTENCY: ⅓ teaspoon per brownie

The creation of this deep-South treat is an inspired way to apply some of your mild-tasting but potent butter. In addition, the recipe produces brownies which are deliciously light in potency. Thus, any of us who can't resist two or three won't be put into the deep sleep.

⅓ cup mild-tasting marijuana butter plus ⅓ cup regular butter
2 ounces bittersweet chocolate
3 large fresh eggs
1 cup sugar
1 teaspoon rum
2 tablespoons molasses or heavy dark honey
1 tablespoon vanilla extract
1 cup unbleached white flour
1 teaspoon sea salt
1 cup pecan pieces
1 cup small marshmallows

1. Melt the butter and chocolate in the top of a double boiler over simmering water.
2. Remove the mixture from the heat, and allow it to cool.
3. Blend the eggs and sugar, and stir into the cooled chocolate/butter mixture.
4. Add the rum, molasses, and vanilla and blend well.
5. Sift together the flour and salt, then add them to the mixture. Stir in the pecans and marshmallows.
6. Grease a 9-by-12-inch pan with butter or shortening. Spread the brownie mixture evenly in the pan and bake in a preheated 325° oven for 20 to 25 minutes, or until a toothpick comes out clean. Cool and then cut into 1½-inch squares.

Colombian Cream

YIELD: Depends on the cake
POTENCY: 24 teaspoons total

The most potent birthday cake icing around. A variation on the recipe developed by a friend in Houston.

½ cup sweet marijuana butter
½ cup fresh milk
1 teaspoon instant coffee powder
2 ounces semisweet chocolate, grated
2 cups turbinado (unrefined) sugar
¼ cup light corn syrup
¼ teaspoon salt
1 teaspoon dark rum

1. Combine all ingredients except the rum in a heavy saucepan. Stir constantly over low heat until the butter and chocolate have melted.
2. Bring the mixture to a rolling boil, stirring all the time. Use medium-high heat if possible.
3. After 60 seconds on rolling boil, remove the saucepan from the heat and set it in 2 to 3 inches of cold water in the sink, stirring even as you transfer it from the stove.
4. Continue stirring vigorously until the mix is lukewarm, then add the rum.
5. Beat until the frosting has achieved spreading consistency. At higher altitudes, use ½ teaspoon more rum.

Black Ganja Mousse

YIELD: 8 servings
POTENCY: 1½ teaspoons per serving

    5 medium or 4 large egg yolks
1¼ cups turbinado (unrefined) sugar
    4 tablespoons grated bitter chocolate
⅔ cup whole milk
¼ cup marijuana butter plus ¾ cup regular butter
    1 tablespoon chocolate liqueur, such as Cherry Suisse
      Grated chocolate for garnish

1. Beat the egg yolks until smooth. Add half the sugar and continue to beat until the sugar has dissolved. Add the grated chocolate.
2. In a heavy saucepan, bring the milk slowly to a low boil, then dribble it into the yolk/sugar mixture, beating briskly with a whisk. Return the mixture to the saucepan, and cook over a very low heat until it thickens nicely.
3. Fill a large bowl one-third full with ice cold water. Put the custard into a smaller bowl, set it into the larger one, and whisk the custard until it has cooled.
4. In another bowl, beat the butter and remaining sugar together until light and fluffy. Add the custard, and beat the mixture until it's smooth and velvety. Swirl in the liqueur with a light touch.
5. Pour the mousse into eight small, attractive mousse dishes, cover, and chill in the refrigerator for four hours or more. Serve cold, topped with an additional bit of grated chocolate.

Eggnog Santa Maria

YIELD: 16 cups
POTENCY: Depends on strength and amount of marijuana used

If you've got a few nice buds and Christmas is just around the corner, try making up a batch of this extra-special nog. And if you think Santa enjoys it when a few cookies are left out for him, just imagine the twinkle that a cup of this high-spirited drink will bring to his eye.

½ pint marijuana whipping cream
½ pint bourbon
 Marijuana buds
¾ cup turbinado (unrefined) sugar
8 egg yolks
12 egg whites, stiffly beaten
 Freshly ground nutmeg

1. Mix the cream and bourbon in the top of a double boiler. Heat over barely simmering water. When hot, remove from the heat and add the buds. Cool the mixture, and then refrigerate, covered, overnight.
2. Blend the sugar and egg yolks together until light and creamy.
3. Skim the film off the chilled cream mixture, then strain to remove the marijuana buds.
4. Stir the cream mixture slowly into the sugar/yolk mixture.
5. Fold in the stiffly beaten egg whites, and sprinkle with nutmeg.

Butter Spreads

Each of these spread recipes presupposes that you have prepared marijuana butter on hand, probably kept in wrapped ice cube trays in the freezer.

Anchovy Butter

YIELD: 24 teaspoons
POTENCY: ½ teaspoon per teaspoon

This potent spread works well with tuna or salmon sandwiches. Use ¼ cup softened marijuana butter with ¼ cup softened regular butter. Squeeze 1 tablespoon fresh lemon juice over the butter, add 3 tablespoons anchovy paste and a few chopped sprigs of parsley. Blend vigorously with a fork, or blend for a few seconds in a food processor.

Horseradish Butter

YIELD: 12 teaspoons
POTENCY: 1 teaspoon per teaspoon

Mix ¼ cup softened marijuana butter with 2 tablespoons prepared horseradish. (If preparing fresh horseradish, add one or two drops of Tabasco sauce.) Blend by hand or in a food processor. This simple spread does wonders for roast beef hors d'oeuvres, cold lamb, or veal.

Butter Picante

YIELD: 12 teaspoons
POTENCY: ½ teaspoon per teaspoon

Combine 2 tablespoons softened marijuana butter and 2 tablespoons softened regular butter. Blend in 1 tablespoon whole-seed French mustard, 1 tablespoon Worcestershire sauce, 1 teaspoon chopped shallot, 1 tablespoon chopped fresh parsley, either by hand or in a food processor. An excellent spread for ham sandwiches.

Red Wine Butter

YIELD: 12 teaspoons
POTENCY: 1 teaspoon per teaspoon

For a completely different sensation, try this over grilled ground beef—preferably a chuck arm you've ground yourself just before cooking. In a non-aluminum pot, over moderate heat, cook 1½ tablespoons minced shallots in 1 cup red wine, until the wine is reduced to half its original volume. Allow the wine to cool. Cream together ¼ cup softened marijuana butter, 1 teaspoon fresh chopped parsley, a chopped sprig of fresh thyme, if available, and the cooled wine mixture. You can do this by dribbling the wine/shallot mixture over the butter and stirring vigorously, or you can blend everything in a processor.

Mushroom Butter with Herbs

YIELD: 12 teaspoons
POTENCY: 1½ teaspoons per teaspoon

Sauté 2 ounces finely chopped mushrooms for two minutes in 2 tablespoons marijuana butter. Add one peeled, smashed but intact clove of fresh garlic, and sauté for another 2 minutes over medium-high heat, taking care not to brown the butter. Remove the pan from the heat and allow to cool. Stir occasionally to aid the cooling process and keep everything moist. After 10 to 15 minutes, remove the garlic clove.

Prepare ¼ cup marijuana butter by blending in the following herbs: 2 tablespoons chopped fresh parsley, 2 teaspoons chopped fresh tarragon or 1 teaspoon dried tarragon, 2 tablespoons chopped fresh or bottled chives, 1 tablespoon whole-seed French mustard, 1 teaspoon brandy, a dash of salt, and a dash of exotic pepper, if available.

Blend the sautéed mushrooms with the butter/herb mixture, turn into a dish, and chill. Use for an esoteric cookout on grilled red meat.

NOTE: You can flavor marijuana butter with herbs simply by adding the herbs, usually in small amounts, to the extract while it's cooking.

Buttered Vegetables

If you enjoy fresh vegetables, you'll find that marijuana butter can be a fine taste complement, and a very light way to become very high. In fact, the colored nonstarchy vegetables seem to take the marijuana butter deep into the body system, where the time-release effects of marijuana foods are accentuated.

Some vegetarian highs we've tried and liked include:

> Steamed artichokes dipped in lemon butter
> Steamed asparagus served with a teaspoon of butter melted over the tips and upper stalks of really fresh, young asparagus dipped in hot lemon butter
> Steamed broccoli served with a teaspoon of butter melted over
> Carrots sautéed with shallots in lemon butter
> Buttered baked potato skins
> Steamed, buttered fresh garden peas, garnished with mint and green onion

Clarified Marijuana Butter

If, instead of using the water bath technique for producing marijuana butter, you want to make small amounts of butter from potent and aromatic sinsemilla buds in a double boiler, you'll want to use clarified butter rather than regular butter.

It's easy to make clarified butter, which has multiple advantages over regular butter: it keeps extremely well and does not burn as easily in recipes calling for high temperatures.

Melt a cup or so of butter in a heavy saucepan over very low heat. Be very sure you don't burn it. When the butter is melted, a foam will be floating on the top. Skim this off and discard it. Then raise the temperature a little. More foam will form. Skim that off and discard it. Repeat the process several times until you get no more foam.

Now, carefully pour off the clear, straw-colored liquid butter, leaving the sediment at the bottom of the pan. You now have clarified butter, which you can process and use for escargot or other dishes calling for this delightful and unique substance.

Hearty Dishes

> Our only way of testing marijuana is to try it on dogs. If the dog's legs get tangled, the drug is potent. If you go on giving the dog marijuana, his brain is destroyed.
> —Harry Anslinger, *Testimony Before Congress During Hearings on the Marijuana Tax Stamp Act*, 1937

Well, we can testify that dogs do love marijuana food leftovers, and platter-licking was never so enthusiastic as when our mongrel pack settled down to the dishes after our dinner party had devoured a heap of Fettuccine à la Santa Marta.

This is one of the few recipes where you can use your greenest butter with abandon—at least, with all the abandon your motor network can handle.

Fettuccine à la Santa Marta

YIELD: 6 to 8 servings
POTENCY: 1½ to 2 teaspoons per serving

Because of the heavy, creamy nature of this dish the high takes a while to come on, but it lasts a long, long time. This is an excellent dish for a long cold evening with friends at home, not one for getting out and playing hard.

> 1½ cups heavy cream
> 6 ounces freshly grated Parmesan cheese
> ¼ cup marijuana butter plus ¼ cup regular butter
> 2 extra-large egg yolks, beaten
>   Salt and freshly ground black pepper
> 1 pound fettuccine noodles
> ½ cup chopped fresh Italian parsley

1. Use a heavy saucepan to slowly heat the cream to a low simmer. Just as the cream comes to a simmer, sprinkle in the Parmesan, stirring constantly. Stir slowly for 8 to 10 minutes to dissolve the Parmesan, then start adding the butter bit by bit.
2. Once all the butter has been added, remove a little of the sauce and set it aside to cool for a minute or so. Then dribble the beaten egg yolks into the smaller amount a little at a time, stirring vigorously. (Never dump egg yolks directly into anything hot unless you want curdled eggs floating around in the sauce.) By incorporating the yolks into a bit of slightly warm sauce and *then* dribbling this mixture slowly into the main body of sauce, whisking gently, you avoid this ugly problem. When the egg yolks are thoroughly mixed in, season lightly with salt and pepper.

   Incidentally, it's a very good idea to grind your own pepper. The pepper you can buy pre-ground is one of the world's filthiest spices. Next to chocolate, pre-ground pepper has the highest average proportion of insect parts

of any foodstuff commonly available. Besides, freshly ground pepper tastes so much better!
3. Bring a big pot of water to a rolling boil, add a little olive oil, salt the water well, and add your noodles. Cook them until they are tender but not soft and soggy. Warm your colander by dunking it into the cooking water, then drain the noodles in the colander. Transfer them to a warmed serving dish, and pour the Santa Marta sauce over them, mixing the noodles to distribute the sauce evenly.
4. Garnish with the chopped parsley, and serve at once.

Sweet Potatoes Bogotá

YIELD: 4 servings
POTENCY: 2 teaspoons per serving

```
  3 small sweet potatoes
  2 organic Valencia oranges
1½ teaspoons ground cinnamon
  3 tablespoons marijuana butter, melted
  1 large fresh egg, beaten
 ¼ teaspoon sea salt
    Mint sprigs for garnish
```

1. Cook the sweet potatoes until they are tender. Peel and mash them.
2. Cut the oranges in half, juice them, and set aside the shells.
3. Blend together the mashed sweet potatoes, cinnamon, half the orange juice, the melted butter, beaten egg, and salt. If necessary, add a bit more juice. You want a mashed-potato consistency.
4. Fill each of the orange shells with mixture, and put them on a cookie sheet.
5. Bake for 12 to 15 minutes in a preheated 400° oven. Remove from the oven and top with a sprig of fresh mint.

Marijuana Rice Patty

Natural brown rice is wonderful stuff. It's the world's most complete single food, it tastes great and complements a vast range of other flavors, it stores well both cooked and uncooked, it's easy to prepare, it's inexpensive, and it's wholesome.

I always prepare a large batch of rice and plan on keeping it in the refrigerator and cooking with it for the next week or so. The older the rice gets, the better it tastes and the more versatile it becomes.

A good water to rice ratio is 1¼ cups of natural brown rice to 3 cups of water. Bring the water to a boil, and add several cubes of homemade stock. You can also use powdered stock base. If you do, add 3 teaspoons more water. Add a pinch or two of salt and 2 or 3 tablespoons of oil. Olive oil, sunflower oil, grapeseed oil, and walnut oil each give the finished rice a distinctive flavor.

Chop a medium yellow onion, not too fine, and add to the boiling water. Dump in the rice, stir for a minute or so with a wooden spoon, cover the pot, and turn the heat down to a mild simmer. Don't lift the lid for 45 minutes, and then peek at your rice. Watch out for the cloud of steam when you first crack the lid.

If there's a lot of liquid still left, cover, and raise the heat slightly for another five minutes. If there's just a little liquid in the bottom, or when it gets to that point, turn the rice gently with your wooden spoon until enough water is evaporated and absorbed that the rice begins to look gluey and slightly translucent, which will take 3 to 10 minutes, depending on how dry the atmosphere is that day.

If you're using electric burners, a wire separator under the cooking pot will help keep food from sticking and burning. The wire separator helps even out the heat reaching the pot bottom, preventing hot spots which cause burning when the pot's in direct contact with the burner. You can buy separators almost anywhere, or you can make one yourself by bending some good 18–20-gauge steel wire into an appropriate shape—a four-sided star works best. No need to solder. (Don't use coathanger wire or other soft wire or it will melt all over your electric burner.)

Once the rice is cooked, set it aside in the pot to cool, then transfer it to a lidded container for storage. For fried rice, it's best to wait at least a day after the original cooking.

So, with your aged rice, here's how to prepare a fantastic marijuana rice dish for as many people as you like:

First, heat a tablespoon of oil in an iron skillet to medium heat. Then toss a handful of raw sunflower seeds in the oil. Even out the seeds in the bottom of the pan, and stir every 15 to 20 seconds. They will brown rapidly.

Just as most of the seeds become visibly brown, put about a cup of rice into the pan, stirring the rice and the sunflower seeds together immediately. This prevents scorching of the seeds. As soon as the rice and seeds are thoroughly mixed, put them into a little pancake in the middle of the skillet, and put the proper amount of marijuana butter (depending on your desired dosage) on top of the little rice cake, allowing it to melt down into the rice. Lift the lip of the rice cake after a minute or so, and when the rice turns a nice crisp hash-brown color, turn the patty. It may come apart, but that's no cause for alarm, just turn the pieces. Cook for about the same length of time as you did the top, then remove from the skillet and serve yourself a delicious treat.

I like to eat my marijuana rice patty with catsup. You might prefer herb vinegar, or lemon or lime juice or soy sauce. Whatever the garnish, this form of brown rice is easy to prepare, extraordinarily nourishing, and very effective.

Oysters Timothy Leary

YIELD: 12 oyster shellfuls
POTENCY: 2¼ teaspoons per shell

Rockefeller has an oyster dish named after him, so we might as well go for a new-age tradition as well. Of course, this is only one of dozens of seafood dishes where marijuana butter makes for a supreme treat.

> 1 quart drained oysters
> lemon juice
> Salt and freshly ground black pepper
> ½ cup marijuana butter, plus 1 tablespoon marijuana butter
> 1 cup finely chopped celery
> ¼ teaspoon Tabasco sauce
> 1 cup catsup
> 2 teaspoons Worcestershire sauce
> 1 clove garlic, crushed
> 12 large oyster shells
> 1 cup fresh rye bread crumbs
> Lemon and orange slices for garnish

1. Cut the oysters in half, and season to taste with the lemon juice, salt, and pepper.
2. Melt ½ cup marijuana butter in a skillet over low heat, adding the celery, Tabasco, catsup, Worcestershire, and garlic. Add the oysters and simmer gently for 15 to 20 minutes.
3. Place mixture in each of the 12 oyster shells.
4. Sauté the bread crumbs in 1 tablespoon marijuana butter till lightly browned. Add more butter, if necessary.
5. Sprinkle the bread crumbs over the mixture in the oyster shells, and top with a dab of the melted marijuana butter used for sautéing.
6. Place the shells on a cookie sheet 6 inches away from the flame until browned nicely. Serve hot garnished with lemon and orange slices.

Refried Cucaracha Beans

YIELD: 4 servings
POTENCY: 1 tablespoon per serving

If Pancho Villa had known about cooking with marijuana, his army might have succeeded in taking over the republic. All that he would have had to do was to send pots of this treat ahead of the troops.

    ½ pound dried black beans
    4 quarts water
    2 yellow onions, 1 chopped and 1 grated
    ¼ cup plus 2 tablespoons marijuana bacon drippings
       (divided)
    1 teaspoon salt
       Grated sharp yellow Cheddar cheese
    ½ teaspoon chopped cilantro or parsley

1. Wash the beans in cold water, removing any floaters and stones.
2. Soak the beans overnight in the 4 quarts water.
3. If necessary, add water in the morning—enough to cover the beans. Add the chopped onion, and simmer in an earthenware pot for several hours, or until the beans begin to soften and their skins begin to wrinkle.
4. Add ¼ cup bacon drippings and ½ teaspoon cilantro and continue to simmer for a total of 3½ hours. Keep the beans covered by adding additional hot water as needed.
5. Add the salt and cook for another 30 minutes. Test for soft doneness, and cook a little longer if needed.
6. Strain off the cooking liquid and reserve it. Melt remaining 2 tablespoons bacon drippings in a skillet, and add the drained beans to the skillet a little at a time. Mash the beans and move them around in the skillet, frying them as they become a heavy paste. Add some of the liquid from time to time to maintain a pasty consistency.
7. Serve the beans hot, with grated onion and cheese sprinkled over the top.

Red Dirt Gumbo

YIELD: 20 servings
POTENCY: 2½ teaspoons per serving

They were growing marijuana in the red dirt country of deep, east Texas, Louisiana, and Arkansas long before the Feds made it illegal in 1937—and they've been growing it there since. Marijuana gumbo can kick like a Mississippi mule, and it's good. Here's a gumbo for the extravagant, for those satisfied with mere perfection. What makes this recipe special is that it uses marijuana bacon fat.

     1 cup marijuana bacon drippings
     ½ cup regular bacon drippings
     3 cups all-purpose unbleached flour
     1 bunch celery, tops removed, chopped
     2 large yellow onions, chopped
     2 pounds fresh okra, chopped
     6 large cloves garlic, crushed
    60 to 80 ounces tomato sauce
     5 pounds medium shrimp, washed, but not shelled, with head and legs removed
     5 pounds crab claws, cracked, but meat left in shell
     1 large bunch scallions, chopped
     1 thick slice sugar-cured ham (an outside slab, with the sugar crust intact), diced
     2 handfuls chopped fresh parsley
     1 handful dried red pepper pods
       Tabasco sauce or Louisiana Hot Sauce
    2½ tablespoons gumbo file dissolved in 1 cup warm water
       Cooked brown, white, or wild rice

1. Melt half the marijuana bacon drippings and all the regular bacon drippings in a cast-iron skillet. When melted, stir in the flour to make a roux.
2. Add the celery, onions, okra, and garlic. Simmer over medium heat for about four minutes, or until the celery is tender.

3. Pour the mixture into a 10- to 12-quart soup pot. Add the tomato sauce, shrimp, crab, scallions, ham, parsley, pepper pods, and Tabasco sauce to taste.
4. Fill the pot with water and bring to a simmer, stirring occasionally. Simmer for about six hours. Add the remaining marijuana bacon drippings from time to time, making sure that the last addition is at least two hours before the end of cooking.
5. When the gumbo has cooked for six hours, lower the heat as low as possible and add the dissolved gumbo file and water. Stir to distribute evenly.
6. Serve in a bowl with steaming rice that has been topped with a little dab of marijuana butter.

Enchilada Oaxacaño

YIELD: 4 servings
POTENCY: 1 tablespoon per serving

To commemorate all those gut-wrenching runs across the border, we've devised this variation on traditional Mexican stacked enchiladas.

      4 tablespoons marijuana bacon drippings
    1½ pounds very lean ground chuck—best it you grind it
          fresh yourself
    1¼ cups enchilada sauce
      ½ cup water
      1 large ripe tomato
      2 medium yellow onions
    1½ pounds mild Cheddar cheese
      2 cups shredded lettuce
          Oil for frying tortillas (You can use marijuana bacon
          drippings if you want to add a little potency.)
    12 corn tortillas

1. Brown the meat in the bacon drippings. When meat is nicely browned, pour the enchilada sauce into the pan, and add the water.
2. Simmer the meat over low heat for 30 minutes.
3. Chop the tomato and onions. Grate the cheese. Set them all aside separately with the shredded lettuce.
4. Heat the cooking oil in another skillet, and fry one tortilla at a time over medium-high heat for 60 seconds each.
5. When all the tortillas have been cooked (keeping the first ones warm in the oven), place a tortilla on a warm plate. Sprinkle with chopped onion and grated cheese. Repeat the process for a second layer, then place a third tortilla on top.
6. Sprinkle the third tortilla liberally with cheese and onion. Pour over a bit of the enchilada sauce. Run the stack under the broiler till the cheese melts, then remove and top with lettuce and tomato. Serve hot.

Cannabis Quiche Lorraine

YIELD: 6 slices
POTENCY: 1 tablespoon per slice

There are two sources of potency in this delicious main dish: the marijuana butter in the crust and the marijuana bacon drippings in the body of the quiche. A tasty dish indeed. The higher potency is to compensate for the stomach-coating qualities of the cheese and cream.

      4 slices cooked bacon
      1 baked 9- or 10-inch Marijuana Pastry Crust (see p. 134)
      1 large yellow onion, sliced
      2 tablespoons marijuana bacon drippings
    ½ cup grated Gruyère cheese
      1 cup minced baked ham
      6 slices aged Swiss cheese, cut into strips
      3 large fresh eggs
    ½ teaspoon French mustard
      1 cup cream, warmed slightly
        Fresh grated nutmeg

1. Crumble the cooked bacon, and spread over the bottom of the pie shell.
2. Gently sauté the onion in the bacon drippings until the onion turns opaque, about four to five minutes.
3. Place the cooked onions over the crumbled bacon, then add half the grated Gruyère cheese. Place half the ham and two slices' worth of the Swiss cheese over that. Pour some of the potent drippings over the whole thing.
4. Repeat layers of ham and cheese, sprinkling remaining Gruyère bit by bit over each layer and moistening each layer with bacon drippings.
5. Beat the eggs and mustard together and add the warmed cream. Pour the mixture into the pan used to sauté the onions. Swish it around, and pour over the contents of the pie shell.
6. Sprinkle grated nutmeg to taste over the top.
7. Bake in a preheated 375° oven for 30 to 35 minutes.

Crusts

Marijuana Pastry Crust for Quiches and Custard Pies

YIELD: 2 9–10-inch crusts
POTENCY: 15 teaspoons per crust

This is an excellent short crust for quiche. It's very light and crumbly, and works well at any altitude. You don't roll out this crust; rather, you pat it into shape in a buttered pie pan or baking dish with buttered fingers.

> 2 cups unbleached white pastry flour
> ⅓ cup marijuana butter plus ⅓ cup regular butter, softened
> Pinch of sea salt
> 1 tablespoon turbinado (unrefined) sugar

1. Sift the flour, salt, and sugar together in a broad bowl. Using a wide-tined fork or a dull dinner knife, blend the butter with the flour mix until you get a coarse, gravellike mixture, then mash it around with well-buttered fingers until you have a nice grainy blend. Don't expect a smooth mixture. Pat the dough into a ball, wrap in a dry clean cloth, and chill in the refrigerator for two hours.
2. Remove the dough from the refrigerator, and pat it flat on an *unfloured* surface. (Whenever you are going to work a crust by hand you don't want to flour it, because that will prevent the pieces from molding together.)
3. Pat the dough out in a circle with thick edges, the size of the pan bottom. Place the dough into the pan, and pinch the dough up the sides of the pan. You may set aside a bit of the dough before beginning so that you'll have a stockpile for repairs to this basic crust.
4. Finish the top edges with nice little scalloped pinches just like on Grandma's apple pie, then prick the crust thoroughly with a fork. Prick all over the bottom and on the

sides. This will prevent bubbling of the crust during pre-baking.
5. Set the oven at 425° to 450°, and, after allowing time for preheating, bake the crust for 10 minutes. You now have a finished crust, which you can fill and continue cooking, or which you can freeze.

Rich Marijuana Pastry Crust for pies and tarts

YIELD: 12 slices
POTENCY: 1 teaspoon per slice

This crust is much richer than the preceding quiche crust.

¼ cup marijuana butter, softened
1 cup whole-wheat pastry flour
1 large egg
2 egg yolks
  Pinch of salt
¼ cup turbinado (unrefined) sugar

1. Blend the butter with the flour until you have a grainy mixture. Blend the egg, yolks, salt, and sugar together, and beat into the flour/butter mixture. Cover and refrigerate for two hours.
2. Work this dough into your pie pan with lightly buttered fingers. Poke holes in the bottom and sides with a fork. Bake in a 400° oven for five to seven minutes if you are going to fill and bake some more, which you would do if you were using this crust in a tart recipe. If you are going to fill a completely baked crust, as in the case of High Lime Pie (p. 112), bake for 20 minutes.

NOTE: This recipe makes one 10-inch crust, with about 1 teaspoon of potency per slice. To cut the potency, use half marijuana butter and half regular butter.

Marijuana Herbal Liqueurs

The delightful taste of sweet sinsemilla can be captured deliciously in any liqueur, but there are several combinations which work like a charm.

Preparing a good marijuana liqueur is a two-stage process. First you must prepare the alcohol extract of marijuana. Vodka makes an excellent base, Scotch is sophisticated, grain alcohol is effective but harsh, tequila oscuro is a treat, and heavy, dark rum is excellent, particularly 181 proof.

First, decide how potent you want your liqueur to be. A ratio of 1 ounce of buds to 1 quart of alcohol base results in a light but effective liqueur. For weaker marijuana, you can use up to 3 ounces of marijuana to a quart of base, or you can make a very potent liqueur by using more than an ounce of high potency buds. If you don't have homegrown sinsemilla, any other good-tasting, good-smelling marijuana will do. The taste of the marijuana you use in making liqueurs is important, so stay away from musty-smelling marijuana and from wild weed.

Heat the alcohol in a double boiler on an electric burner. Remember, you can't heat alcohol on an electric burner and you can never use a gas burner. When the alcohol comes to a slow simmer, add the marijuana and a pinch of powdered Vitamin C (ascorbic acid). Don't use a crushed Vitamin C pill, but instead use pure crystalline Vitamin C available in most health food stores or pharmacies. The Vitamin C helps keep your extract base clear; without it you often get a muddy brown liquid. After adding the Vitamin C, turn off the heat. Pour the mixture into either a large canning jar, or better yet, into a large-capacity Thermos. Put the cap on tight, and set the jug aside for 24 hours. After that, add the syrup we'll describe shortly, let it mellow for a week or two with the marijuana in, and then decant it into a jar and set the marijuana aside. The tincture in the jar is now the marijuana alcohol extract.

The marijuana you've set aside should not be thrown

away. For reasons unknown, the tincture extraction process just described sometimes absorbs all the potency of the marijuana, while other times it absorbs most but not all of it, and the buds remain potent enough to make quite respectable marijuana butter.

After producing the tincture, you must decide whether to make it sweet, to add other flavors, or to leave it as it is. To make an easy, classic sweet liqueur base, take equal parts of honey and water. Heat the water to a boil, remove it from the heat, and stir in the honey. Be discriminating about the honey you use. Many supermarket honeys have little taste and sweetness. That's because the bees have been fed on sugar and water only—no flowers. Many other honeys may have a taste which works well on toast but is a disaster in blend with the flavors of the food it's sweetening. A good organic clover, sage, tupelo, or orange blossom honey will usually work well. By the way, when measuring honey, if you first coat the spoon or cup lightly with a bland oil, like safflower, the honey will all pour right out.

Now to think about which herbs to add to the liqueur . . . If you've had the pleasure of growing your own herbs, you need no prompting to use fresh herbs in every endeavor. If you don't have any fresh herbs on hand and want to try a few good marijuana herbal liqueurs right away, there are many flavorings which you can use instead of fresh herbs.

Prepare the herbs for flavoring in the appropriate way. Generally, fresh aromatic leaves are lightly crushed in the fingers, seeds are ground till cracked but not reduced to a powder with a mortar and pestle, peels are lightly bruised with a wooden mallet on a cutting board. Place the herb in a heatproof glass jar and add a pinch of vitamin C. Then, heat the alcohol as described for the marijuana base, using the same precautions, and pour over the prepared herb till it's just covered with hot alcohol. Close the jar and let the mixture set for 24 hours in the dark.

After the 24-hour blending period, uncap the alcohol marijuana tincture and add the herbal alcohol tincture, and the sweet syrup if you intend to do so, then reclose the Thermos and let it stand for 10 to 14 days.

Orange, lemon, and grapefruit peels are such wonderful flavoring ingredients. It's always important to use skins from fruit grown without toxic sprays, and packaged without toxic dyes, because the liqueur-making process will concentrate these chemicals right along with the essential oils and essence of the citrus peel. A couple of delicious liqueurs using orange peel follow.

Marijuana Marin

Fennel grows wild in many parts of the country, but nowhere so prolifically as in northern California. Marijuana Marin is an appropriate name for this mellow liqueur.

Take 2 tablespoons of sun-dried fennel seed, and crush lightly with a mortar and pestle to release the aroma.

Take the peel of ½ orange, preferably a ripe, sweet organically grown Valencia, and slice into ¼-inch strips. Bruise with a mallet, but don't crush.

Put the fennel and orange peel into a jar or Thermos bottle, and sprinkle in a pinch of vitamin C. Cover the contents with warm alcohol, close the jar or Thermos tight, and set aside for 24 hours.

After 24 hours, pour the mixture into the prepared marijuana base (vodka is best), along with honey/water syrup to taste—approximately 1 cup will do for 1 quart of fresh alcohol—and steep for two weeks. After two weeks, strain off the liquid and store it in a dark bottle in a cool but not cold place. This is a nice dessert liqueur with custards and pies.

Marijuana Mint

It's so easy to grow a little mint, particularly in the spring and summer in a cool, moist place around the house, that it's hard to imagine anyone who can't get some nice fresh mint to use in making this fine cordial.

Use 3 tablespoons fresh crushed peppermint or orange mint leaves, 1 tablespoon lightly crushed caraway seeds, and the lightly bruised peel of ½ organic orange, cut into ¼-inch strips. Sprinkle all with a pinch of vitamin C.

Steep in hot alcohol for 24 hours in a closed heatproof jar, using enough alcohol to cover.

After 24 hours, strain off the liquid and discard the fennel seed, the mint, and the peels. Add the liquid to the appropriate amount of marijuana alcohol base (vodka is best), depending on your own taste for the right proportion. Then add 1 tablespoon fresh crushed mint to the marijuana base mix. Add honey/water syrup to taste, in the ratio of about 1 cup syrup to 1 quart alcohol, then set the whole thing aside to steep for two weeks. Finally, filter out all the flavoring herbs, and store the liqueur in a dark bottle in a cool dark place.

Highland Fling

When the Scots gave us Scotch, it's unlikely that they were thinking about whether or not it makes a good base for marijuana liqueur, but with the right luck in mating marijuana to whiskey blend or, better yet, to the proper taste of malt Scotch whiskey, you can produce a fine liqueur reminiscent of Drambuie, the drink devised by the Bonnie Prince Charlie.

Smell your buds to get an idea of whether you want a light Scotch blend like J&B or a heavy malt whiskey like Glenfiddich. Then make 1 pint of marijuana base, using 1 ounce sinsemilla buds and 1 pint Scotch whiskey of your choice.

Prepare 2 tablespoons crushed aniseed, sprinkle with a pinch of vitamin C, and cover with hot Scotch, and allow to steep in a closed heatproof jar overnight.

Next day, add ½ cup honey syrup, the steeped aniseed and its liqueur to the pint of marijuana base. Steep closed for two weeks, then decant, carefully straining out the tiny aniseed using several layers of cheesecloth.

Store the liqueur in a dark bottle in a cool dark place.

Tequilajuana

Many people are going to prefer tequila to any other alcohol base for marijuana, and its woody aroma with a suggestion of lemon makes an excellent background for marijuana liqueur.

Take 2 to 3 ounces of fine buds and pack them into a 1½-quart Thermos bottle. Heat 1 quart of good tequila (not the cheap stuff) in a double boiler as described earlier.

Sprinkle a pinch or two of vitamin C over the buds, then pour the hot tequila over them, and close the Thermos. Allow to stand and blend for two weeks. After two weeks, drain off the emerald aromatic tequila, and store it in a dark bottle in a cool dark place.

Don't forget—don't throw away the marijuana. Test a little of it to see if you can make marijuana butter with it. (See p. 82 for small-batch testing procedures.)

Lemon Ganja Brandy Liqueur

Brandy also makes a good base for marijuana liqueurs, but it will do a better job of picking up the potency if it is blended half and half with a good vodka.

Make 1 pint marijuana brandy extract using 1 ounce sinsemilla buds, ½ pint brandy, and ½ pint vodka. Sprinkle with a pinch of powdered vitamin C. Heat to a low simmer in a double boiler.

Add ¾ cup fresh lemon-balm leaves, lightly crushed. You may substitute the fresh peel of one-half of an organic, unsprayed lemon if you want, but lemon balm has a subtlety which is nice to get. Decant into a large Mason jar and allow to cool. Steep for 24 hours, then filter.

Add ¾ cup honey syrup to the marijuana brandy base. Allow to stand closed for two weeks. Refilter the liquid and store in a dark bottle in a cool dark place.

CHAPTER *9*

Home Growing for Home Cooking

In this chapter we'll cover one basic, trustworthy approach to growing a couple of fine marijuana plants indoors under lights. After two months, each carefully tended plant will yield ½ ounce or so of increasingly tasty potent pickings every other week, and at maturity will also yield several sinsemilla harvests of an ounce or more.

Of course, there are many ways to grow marijuana indoors and outdoors. The method we'll cover here works well almost anywhere—in a corner or closet, on a bench in the basement, on a patio or balcony—anywhere that's secure. Please remember that growing your own marijuana is legal only in Alaska. As of 1981, in 30 states it is a felony to grow even a single plant of your own, while it's only a misdemeanor to possess small quantities of marijuana you've bought from a dealer. In other words, if you patronize the system, you get off easy; but if you try for independence, you get heavy treatment and years in jail. It's worth remembering that the marijuana business consists not only of the folks who bring it in and sell it, but also of tens of thousands of police, judges, and bureaucrats who deal with drug arrests and collect in fees and salaries hundreds and thousands of dollars each year. All that money being made on both sides of the law depends on marijuana's continued illegality, and on a steadily growing market for $50-an-ounce weed.

So if you decide to grow your own, do it in a safe place, and *don't* talk about what you're doing or show your plants off to friends.

But if all you want is a simple approach to growing first-class marijuana on a small scale, here's how to proceed.

Step 1.   Select good seed. Seed from marijuana that got you very stoned will produce plants that do the same. Marijuana that got you high instead of stoned will produce light but potent offspring. Don't pay a lot of money for special seed unless you know the grower personally.

Step 2.   Obtain good soil. Either use topsoil from a garden or buy a good soil from a nursery. An excellent soil mixture is five parts sifted garden soil, three parts crushed lava or pumice stone (you can use sand), and one part aged compost or manure. If quarts are your unit of measure, 5 quarts sifted soil, 3 quarts pumice or clean sand, and 1 quart aged compost or manure will make slightly more than 2 gallons of excellent growing medium, enough for one larger container like the one I describe in Step 5. Mix or buy the amount of soil you need for the number of plants you intend to grow. Keep your soil mixture in a pile outside, or store it in a heavy-duty plastic trash bag.

Step 3.   Check the soil's acidity/alkalinity level if there is reason to believe that the soil is very acid. Soil from a chemically fertilized vegetable garden is often highly acidic. Also, store-bought soil may contain a lot of bark or peat moss, either of which produces acidity. Sudbury puts out an excellent soil-testing kit with full instructions for under $10. If your soil tests below 7.0, raise the pH level with ⅛ cup of dolomite (powdered limestone) per quart. Dolomite is available in most nursery supply stores. Just mix the dolomite into the pile of soil, and let it sit for a couple of weeks.

Step 4.   Whether or not the soil's pH level needs adjusting, it's a good idea to add ½ cup of a good time-release fertilizer for every 2 gallons of soil you prepare, and to let the soil sit for a few weeks, watering it and turning the pile or shaking the bag occasionally. This cures the soil mixture and will result in better plant growth. When choosing a time-release fertilizer, look for a well-balanced formula such as a 12-12-12 or 20-20-20.

Step 5.   For each plant you plan to raise to maturity you will need two 15- to 18-inch diameter large plastic pots. So, say you're raising two plants—you'll need four pots. Take two of the pots and cut the bottoms off. Next, take the two intact pots and place 3 to 4 inches of coarse gravel or broken clay pot pieces in the bottom. This layer promotes drainage and helps keep air flowing through the soil. Then fill these pots to the brim with your cured soil mixture. Drench with water, and add more soil to bring the soil level back up to the brim.

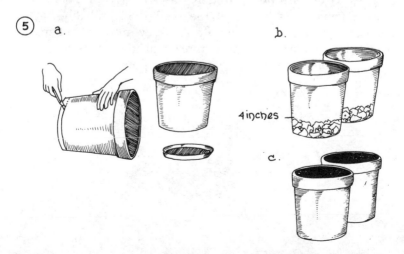

Step 6. Next push the bottomless pots well into the dirt in the filled pots, working the bottomless pots back and forth until they are buried 4 inches or so into the dirt. Then fill these top pots with your cured soil and drench.

Step 7. Soil temperature is the third most important factor in producing excellent marijuana, next to the genetics of the plant and the quality of the light it receives. The ideal soil temperature for marijuana plants is 62° to 65° Fahrenheit. Set your assembled two-tier pots in a warm location, and after a couple of days, check the temperature. Since regular medi-cine-cabinet thermometers don't measure temperatures in the 60s, and since few of us have a soil thermometer around, you will have to do a bit of guesswork. A soil which has stabilized at 65° will not feel the least bit chilly when you stick a finger into it, but it won't feel exactly warm, either. If you can afford about $25 per plant, you can buy one of sev-eral food-warming trays on the market which will produce a near-perfect soil temperature. Put one tier-potted plant in each tray, and set the tray on low.

Step 8. Soak 20 seeds per pot overnight in room-tempera-ture water. In the morning, wet several layers of paper tow-els, and place the soaked seeds in the middle. Leave the seeds in the paper towels for 36 hours, moistening the towels with a sprayer several times.

Step 9. After 36 hours, drench the soil in your pots and inspect your seeds. Some of the seeds will probably have begun to sprout and some won't. Working in a dimly lit area, using clean tweezers, gently transfer all the seeds to scat-tered locations on top of the soil in your pots.

Step 10. Sprinkle about ¼ inch of fine dirt on top of your seeds, and moisten with a sprayer. Repeat as necessary. Within several days, seedlings will begin to emerge.

Step 11. The seedlings should be greeted by a glowing light system. An excellent basic system is a dual-bulb 48-inch fluorescent fixture with the special plant-growing bulbs available almost everywhere—discount stores, nurseries, etc. The 48-inch Gro-Lux VHO bulbs work very well, but brand name is not terribly important. One 48-inch fixture will light two tier-potted plants throughout their lifetimes. Suspend the fixture on a chain or rope, hanging the light about 3 inches above the top of the emerging seedlings. Keep raising the light as the plants grow, maintaining the 3-inch distance.

Step 12. Don't overwater, but don't ever let the soil dry out, either. Keep the top several inches barely moist. With tier potting and good moisture-holding soil, you will need to water only occasionally. If your area is very dry and the top of your pot dries out while the deeper soil stays wet, use a mulch on top of the pot to reduce evaporation. It is *critical* that your plant's roots not be too wet.

Step 13. After your seedlings are about seven days old, select the five best looking ones, and cut the other plants off at soil level with a very sharp blade. If two strong plants are very close to each other, keep only one.

leave five plants

Step 14. Monitor moisture and soil temperature, raise the light fixture, but otherwise just let the plants grow. It's convenient to have the lights on a timer. If you are using one, set the timer for 16 hours of light a day. Be sure to check moisture in both the top and bottom pots. Mist your seedlings occasionally.

Step 15. When the five plants per pot are about 6 inches tall, choose the best two and cut down the rest. A week or so later, cut down one more plant, leaving the strongest, most beautiful one alone in the pot.

leave one plant

Step 16. Continue monitoring soil moisture, and water when necessary. After six weeks of growth, begin watering principally around the rim of the bottom pot. Keep the soil in the upper pot barely moist, and the deep soil moist but not wet. A tip: Young marijuana plants are very vulnerable to overwatering, but if you're growing them in pots, there's a sure-fire way to test the moisture content of your pots. Simply prepare one extra pot with identical soil and drainage, water it every time you water your babies, and if you have any doubts that the soil surrounding your young plants is moist enough, just dig around in the pot without a plant to check the moisture. Until a little plant is four to six weeks old, it won't exert enough water drain on the soil to make it any less moist than the soil in the unplanted test pot.

Step 17.   Maintain control over your plant's profile and stimulate its production of leaves and, ultimately, of flowers by pinching off the growing tips beginning when the plant is about 24 inches high. At this point, take a razor blade and cut off the top 4 to 6 inches of the plant. Also, using sharp scissors, trim off about a quarter of each of the large fan leaves at the base of the plant. Water well and lower the light fixture.

cut off 4-6"

b

cut tips off bottom leaves

Step 18.   After clipping, the plant will begin to put out new growth all over. This is a good time to add an incandescent plant light on both sides of each plant. If you don't want to get this fancy, simply set a lamp with a 150-watt bulb without the shade beside your plants.

Step 19.   Continue monitoring basic plant needs. About every 10 to 14 days, clip back the top of the plant and any prominent new side growth. Don't remove all the new growth in any one area, and rotate the area you groom. Any part of the plant should not be cut more often than every 21 days. The plant can be maintained in growth, and will increase in size and bushiness, without going to flower for an indefinite period by a continuous 16- to 18-hour day and moderate grooming.

Step 20.   When you want to bring on flowering in order to harvest some lovely sticky flowering tops, gradually begin shortening the day length by about 10 to 15 minutes a day until you reach 11 hours a day.

Step 21. Your plants may have begun flower development already, before you've begun to shorten the day length. In either case, as soon as flowers begin to develop and you see a harvest coming on, you need to add a heavy ultraviolet component to the light the plants are receiving. Set up one 150-watt sunlamp per plant, about 4 to 5 feet away. If you

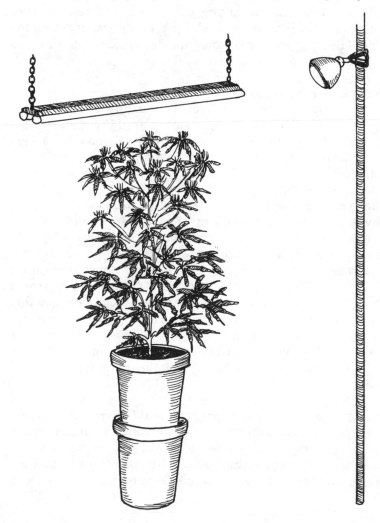

use a clamp-on fixture, be sure it has a heavy-duty porcelain socket to handle the heat, and be sure it is sturdily mounted. Turn on the sunlamps midway through each plant's day, beginning with 30 minutes a day at midday, increasing gradually to 4 hours midday exposure over the course of several weeks. You should also fertilize the lower pot with a high potassium soluble fertilizer.

Step 22. Gradually harvest the flowering heads as they reach full blossom by cutting with a sharp blade or, if your stems are thick, with clean, sharp pruning shears. Hang the individual branches in a temperate dark place, such as a ventilated closet, for two to four weeks.

Step 23. When the cores of the flower clusters on the ends of your hanging branches are dry, no further air-curing is possible. If you dislike the green color and, if you smoke, the acrid taste of air-cured marijuana, you can produce a very nice brown leaf with a much better flavor and smoother smoke by following Jerry's Cure, developed by a genius from the heart of tobacco country. Place a couple of freshly cut flowering tops with all the large and medium leaves removed loosely in a 1-quart canning jar. Reverse the inner lid so that the gasket side is up, and screw the lid on very loosely until you just begin to feel resistance to any further turning. Put the jar in a pressure cooker and cook the flowering tops for an hour at 15 pounds pressure. For each additional jar in a cooker, add five minutes cooking time. To cure leaves rather than tops, screw the lid on just a shade tighter and cook for 45 minutes at 15 pounds pressure. As you can see, growing your own marijuana is a simple process, although many people enjoy making it an art by elaborating upon technique and equipment.

The marijuana plant, acting as a transformer of the light of our sun, a star, into the energy of mind alteration, deserves care and respect. When we are cultivating this ancient green plant, whether in our garden or in a room, on the roof or in a mountain valley, each of us is better able to appreciate the high experience if we first appreciate that this plant has a central role in the evolution of consciousness on the planet. This thoughtful awareness, added to the simple knowledge required to grow the plant, is invaluable in the full cultivation of marijuana.

Conclusion

The use of marijuana should not be an issue. It should be a matter of personal choice. It is an issue only because of outdated laws and because mind-changing substances have eternally aroused fear and anger. In our tradition, a thing as simple as a sneeze needs a blessing, because there is a tiny moment in each sneeze when the mind is somewhere else, when awareness is altered. (Medieval churchmen noticed that they spaced out for just a millisecond when they sneezed, and feared that the devil might slip into control of their minds while they were thus temporarily distracted from their doctrine.) Marijuana is a lot more potent than a sneeze, but the principles which arouse fear and anger, and inspire protective blessings, remain the same. A lot of folks are just plain afraid that anything that does funny things to the mind, that is, any *substance* that does funny things to the mind, is dangerous.

Unfortunately, there is a long, dishonorable tradition in this country of oppressing people who indulge in activities that other people fear to practice on themselves. This means that marijuana is likely to remain a scary phenomenon for quite a while, perhaps forever, in the minds of those people who also dislike so many other human diversions and pleasures.

Marijuana extract cooking offers an alternative not only to smoking, but also to being smoked out by the eternally vigilant as you sit puffing your fiendish weed, sipping mineral water, and thinking altered thoughts.

I hope that this book provides you and your friends with a useful new perspective on marijuana and opens new directions for its use. Above the entrance to the temple of the great Oracle at Delphi were carved two commands: "Know thyself" and "Everything in moderation." This last, presumably, includes moderation itself. Enjoy, dear Reader!

Index